Praise for
THE BIG BOOK OF BAD DECISIONS

"Scott Nathan's life reads like an east of Doheny *Curb Your Enthusiasm*. I'm not sure how he's made so many bad decisions, but I'm glad he did so we can be entertained!"

— Zooey Deschanel

"Scott Nathan has been regaling me with his unspeakably filthy, raucous stories for decades now. I always wonder how he gets himself in these predicaments, but the truth is, he's a natural born misfit-magnet."

— Dita Von Teese

"I thought there was no way this redhead could get into so much mischief and debauchery but, lo and behold… it's all true. I often refer to Scott as a more charismatic, slightly more articulate Forrest Gump."

— Jack Osbourne

"I've known Scott Nathan for years and, I have to say, he has an almost preternatural gift for making bad decisions."

— Dr. Drew Pinsky

"Nathan can't throw for shit, but he's the only guy I know who can smash 100 MPH fastballs while on mushrooms. Great read!"

— Brad Penny,
World Series Champion Pitcher

"At the CIA we laugh and cringe simultaneously—making Scott Nathan a national asset. Read this book and laugh until you cry. It's your patriotic duty."

— Laura Ballman,
Former CIA Operations Officer

"After knowing Scott for years and reading his stories, I've come to realize he's a real deal rodeo cowboy trapped in a photographer's body."

— Luke Branquinho,
5x World Steer Wrestling Champion

"Nathan lights like Caravaggio, writes like Hemingway, and screws like Siffredi."

— Charlotte Sartre,
AVN Award Winner,
Most Outrageous Sex Scene

baddecisionsbook.com

THE BIG BOOK
OF BAD DECISIONS

THE BIG BOOK OF BAD DECISIONS

SCOTT MICHAEL NATHAN

baddecisionsbook.com

- TikTok @scottnathanphoto
- Instagram @scottnathanphoto
- Facebook @scottnathanphoto
- X Twitter @scottnathan

To bad decisons.

CONTENTS

PREFACE

You know that sign in the airplane lavatory that says "In consideration of other passengers, please wipe the basin for the person after you?" That is generally how I've tried to live my life. Considerate and putting others first.

I am a plus-one. An insider outsider. A survivor. I am a cockroach. Easy to hurt. Hard to kill. I never really fit in anywhere. A skinny, left handed, redheaded Jew with few natural skills for navigating childhood. I hated most kid things. I hated superhero comic books and most children's toys and games. I read business magazines. I took pictures when it wasn't a thing.

"Bedtime Stories for Grownups" was the original title for this book. I had to ditch it since there are other books with that title. This was never meant to be a commercial undertaking. It was to make my friends laugh on social media and offer a splash of catharsis.

The original title came as a result of writing some of these dispatches in varying stages of Ambien blackout. I've suffered from insomnia my entire life and depression for most of it. The stories were loose, loud, messy, honest and, for whatever reason, they seemed to resonate with my friends—and, in short order, tens of thousands of strangers.

The routine was consistent. I'd wake up in the morning to figure out what I had eaten in my sleep. I'd look around my bedside and feel relieved not to see any plates in my bed. Then I'd walk to the kitchen to pull a two shots of black Neapolitan espresso only to discover another empty pint container of chocolate Haagen Dazs in the sink.

Mornings would bring anxiety. What did I do? Who did I text? I'd light a cigarette and pour the bitter, tarry liquid into my face as I opened Facebook on my phone. One morning, I woke up to 257 ikes and 79 comments on how I lost my virginity.

Now, I wake up to often thousands, thanks to TikTok. (I don't trust them any more or less than I trust Mark Zuckerberg or Elon Musk, so really, what's the difference?)

My friends and strangers encouraged me to keep going and to compile these into a book.

I think the primary reason I never took it seriously is because, unlike photography, storytelling came easily to me. Looking back, much of my family were raconteurs. As some are born singers, I'm a born storyteller.

Most interestingly, I noticed that I was effecting change. Others in my sphere began to feel safe owning their truths and similar confessions, often in my same patchwork formatting, which I don't mind. They stopped flexing as much. They began finding the humor in life's curveballs, embarrassments and humiliations.

This book is designed very deliberately to be nonlinear and read with today's (my) attention span in mind. Depending on your diet, you should be able to read any of these in the time it takes to go to the bathroom, wait to be called into a doctor's office, or wait in line to board a flight.

So, here we go.

DISCLAIMER

This book of autobiographical short stories, titled "The Big Book of Bad Decisions," is a personal account of the my experiences, thoughts, and opinions. The content within this book is provided for informational and entertainment purposes only.

The author acknowledges that the events and incidents described in this work are based on my recollection and perspective, and as such, may be subject to memory, interpretation, and personal bias. The author does not claim that the events depicted are wholly accurate or complete representations of reality.

Readers are advised to exercise their own judgment and discretion when interpreting and evaluating the content of this book. Any reliance on the information or narratives contained within should be done so with the understanding that this is a subjective account.

The author and publisher disclaim any liability for any consequences, misunderstandings, or disputes that may arise as a result of the content in this memoir. This book does not constitute professional advice or factual reporting, and it should not be used as a primary source of information.

By reading this book, you acknowledge that you have read and understood this disclaimer and that you will use the content within this book responsibly and at your own discretion.

THE BIG BOOK OF BAD DECISIONS

"

*I now run background
checks on every date.
I don't care who you know.*

Chapter One

The Con Woman

F our and a half years ago, I received a friend request on Facebook. Now, normally, I don't accept these from strangers. This woman and I, however, shared 54 mutual friends, and most of them not the traditional friend-hoarder types. I accepted, and over the course of several months we would chat at night with no mention or plan ever to meet. Just passing the time and joking around.

Four or five months in, she messaged me mid-week, just before 10 p.m.

MARY: Hey. I'm in your neighborhood. Want to meet for a drink?

ME: Sure. I'll meet you at The Pikey on Sunset in 15.

We sipped Hendricks and tonics with cucumber and chatted for a couple of hours.

MARY: Let's go to your place and play.

Well, that was easy.

ME: Good idea.

So, we did. No sleepover. She had her dog at home and took off just after 2 a.m. Fine.

This recurred periodically and, by periodically, I mean she would rarely text *me* back, but would hit me up when she had the itch. Typically, three times per year. Fine. The last time I saw her was at her place. A rustic home nestled deep in Nichols Canyon in the Hollywood Hills.

A-frame construction, a big stone fireplace, a small kidney-shaped dipping pool with a waterfall. The kind of home I'd hope to own one day. During that last slumber party, I'd asked about her business, which from outward appearances must be pretty good.

Her business, as she described it, was a well-organized dog-walking agency. She claimed a small fleet of Suburbans, many clients, and their dogs. Knowing half this town's dogs eat better than I do, it seemed plausible. No red flags, but I didn't really care anyway, since we weren't what I'd call dating.

Five months went by before I heard from Mary again. It was on a Monday afternoon.

MARY: (Flustered) Hey, I just had a falling out with my landlord and had to move out. Can I come stay with you for a few days?

ME: I'm kind of seeing someone and it wouldn't be appropriate.

The truth was, despite sleeping with her a handful of times, I didn't know her. She was dodgy. She hadn't done anything overtly suspicious, but I just didn't trust her. Nor did I want a multi-day houseguest with a pit bull.

MARY: Scott. I am literally on the street with no money, my suitcase, and my dog. I have nowhere to go!

ME: Where are you?

MARY: Chatsworth.

ME: Chatsworth? Are you doing porn?

MARY: No! Why does everyone keep asking me that?

I had once read that 77 percent of the world's pornography is produced in the San Fernando Valley, and half of that in the city of Chatsworth.

ME: Where exactly are you? Which intersection?

MARY: De Soto and Devonshire.

ME: (Typing into Google Maps) Do you see the Travelodge?

MARY: Yes, but I have no money.

I wanted this off my plate and was willing to pay to minimize brain damage.

ME: I just booked you three nights there. On me. You don't have to pay me back. Good luck.

Drama avoided. I'd blown $300 faster than that in my life. I neither expected, nor desired, to hear from Mary ever again. If you have had to move out at a moment's notice, then I really don't need to hear the rest of the story. Chances are, you aren't what I'm after.

My first rule in dating is you must be less fucked up than me in every way. A low bar, but it's a start.

To my surprise, four days later I got an email PayPal notification that she had reimbursed me for the motel room. Pretty stand up.

Thirty minutes later, she called.

MARY: Did you get the money?

ME: Yes. Thank you. I said you didn't have to pay me back though.

MARY: I know, but I wanted to. You were there for me when no one else was. I want to do something nice for you.

As I mentioned above, I was now wary of this one…

ME: Totally unnecessary. Just take care of yourself.

MARY: No really, I want to. Now that my trust fund has come through, I'm set for life. I have a patio suite at the Hotel Bel-Air. I'm going to be living here until I find a house to buy.

Whiskey Tango Foxtrot? How does a woman who couldn't swing a motel in Porn Valley a few days ago now afford a nearly $3,000-per-night suite at the best hotel in Los Angeles? This reeked of bullshit. I can smell money on people. Even if they're broke, low-key junkies. You can tell by how people speak and carry themselves.

ME: Great hotel. Great spa.

MARY: Come visit. Stay as long as you like. Eat whatever you want. Get some spa treatments. My treat.

On one hand, I didn't believe her. On the other, I lived only 15 minutes from the H.B.A. I could use a swim, a massage, and a meal. If it turned out to be BS, it was no great time investment.

I threw a few things in a bag, took a left onto Sunset Boulevard, and drove west to the lush, wooded canyons of Bel-Air. This is my favorite part of Los Angeles. Some people prefer the beach. I like old-growth trees. If you've seen what I look like, you'll know why I prefer shade.

I headed to reception and, to my surprise, they were expecting me. They handed me a key card, and a staffer walked me to the suite. She texted that she was out running errands but to enjoy the place. There was a fruit basket and a sealed bottle of Veuve in an ice bucket.

I called the spa. They were able to take me right away. I got a two-hour aromatherapy massage and a facial, followed by a turkey club by the pool while reading Capstick's *Death in the Long Grass*. I headed back to the room for a nap only to be awoken a short while later by everyone's favorite alarm clock. The blowjob.

I stayed two more days, then got bored. I missed my cat, it was all too relaxing, and I couldn't get any work done. Champagne problems, I know, but Mary and I were square.

Another few days went by before I heard from her again.

MARY: It was so great having you! Have you spent any time in Montecito?

ME: Yes. I love Montecito.

Montecito, if you're unfamiliar, is a stunning seaside enclave on the south end of Santa Barbara. It is geographic Valium. Idyllic. It is so devoid of stress that not only is there parking everywhere, they don't even have parking meters. All the restaurants are great and none of them are chains. No one ever asks you for change or a cigarette, and unlike Malibu, they had the forethought not to build a freeway on the fucking beach. If you have ceaseless money and nothing whatsoever to do, it's about as good as you can do in Southern California.

MARY: Do you think I should buy here? My attorney said I can spend up to $10 million on a home.

I was still rolling my eyes, but whatever...

ME: I think it's a great place to live.

MARY: Do you want to come house shopping with me?

ME: Nah. I can't. I have too much work to do. Editing six different shoots and I'm backed up.

MARY: Have you been to Bacara Resort?

ME: Yes. A few times. Golf at Sandpiper and weddings.

MARY: How about this? I'll get you your own suite. You can stay as long as you like and focus on your work. If you have time to see me for a breakfast or dinner, I'll be here.

ME: You don't have to do all of this.

MARY: Scott. I have an almost unspendable amount of money and I want to do nice things for you.

I told her I'd let her know if I could make it.

My next call was to my friends Charlotte and Jeff, a married couple who live in Montecito. I explained the situation and asked if I could stay with them that night if it didn't work out. They said "Of course," and reminded me that I have keys to their guest house and an open invitation.

So off I went. North on the Ventura Freeway, past Montecito proper and downtown Santa Barbara to the less desirable Goleta, to the quite desirable Bacara Resort and Spa. Like the Bel-Air, it was "Welcome, Mr. Nathan" and I was driven in a golf car to my massive suite in the front row, footsteps from the glittering Pacific. Increasingly more comfortable with being spoiled, I opened the chocolate-covered almonds and a mini bottle of Jameson and took a walk on the beach. I had texted Mary a few hours before that I had arrived and checked in, but I hadn't heard from her. Even better.

I stayed there for three weeks to the tune of God knows how much money. Long enough to be almost tired of being fussed over. I didn't want another massage and had eaten everything on their restaurant and room service menus multiple times. I ordered a bottle of Yamazaki 18, a Japanese whisky that supposedly rivaled all but Scotland's very best. It was a bit peaty for me, but whatevs. I then downloaded the SpeedWeed app and had a couple of joints delivered.

I'd had enough. I was going to head home the following day. I called my Montecito friends and invited them and their kids to come have a pool day. We drank smoothies, ate pizza, swam, and got crispy in the sun. At sunset, I took some Yamazaki and ice in a paper coffee-cup with a plastic lid from the room and one of the conical, brown-paper-wrapped pre-rolls from the delivery girl and we walked to the pier.

I woke up early the next morning. Around 8 a.m. I rang the front desk and asked them to wash my car and have it ready by 10:30. Plan was to be back in LA by lunchtime.

I was happy to be home. The next evening, my friend Charlotte from Montecito called.

CHARLOTTE: Where are you?

ME: Back in LA. Had enough of robe life.

CHARLOTTE: Did you hear about Mary?

ME: Hear what? I haven't spoken to her since last night.

CHARLOTTE: Dude. We were having a sunset drink and ran into her. Minutes later she was tackled and handcuffed by a phalanx of FBI agents at the bar at the Four Seasons Biltmore. They arrested her and took her dog away.

ME: You're full of shit. For what?

CHARLOTTE: Google this name.

I did as instructed and sure enough, there were dozens of articles about Mary. One was a listicle of the most notorious con women in American history. This list included women dating back to the 1800s. Mary had been in and out of prison since 1994.

Now I was in a full-blown panic. I was thinking about this whole trip. They knew who I was. My car was at their valet. I had given a copy of my driver's license for incidentals upon check in. I was expecting the Feds at my door any minute. I set Google alerts with her name and the arrest, and waited. When the articles began to pour in, I called my lawyer and told him this whole story.

ME: Phil. Do I need to get ahead of this? Should I call the FBI agent who did the news conference?

PHIL: Scott. The FBI is not your friend. If you call the FBI on yourself, I'm going to drive over to your house and kick you in the balls as hard as I can. Do not call *anyone*. You didn't do anything. If they arrest you, don't say a fucking word. If they call, we'll meet them together. And remember, every syllable you utter to law enforcement, without me, handicaps our ability to do anything.

I didn't sleep for a week.

My friend Gwen produces a 50-state network-news show on crime. I told her what happened. She sent a camera crew down to Mary's arraignment, then texted me a photo of Mary in a royal-blue inmate uniform. Mary had a black eye and a split lip.

Gwen is a Southern lady. Her first text was:

GWEN: (With the obligatory laughing crying emoji) Looks like someone had some sass mouth down at the jailhouse.

I never heard from Mary, the cops, or the FBI. Mary was sentenced to six years in prison for identity theft and a slew of other crimes. She was released early after just two-and-a-half years, due to prison overcrowding and being a nonviolent offender. Thankfully, I haven't heard from her.

I now run background checks on every date. I don't care who you know.

"

*Fine. It was over.
I wasn't a virgin anymore
and I went home.*

Chapter Two

Pink Floyd, the Ferrari, and the Clap

How did you lose your virginity?

It's a question I've always liked to ask people—friends, women, men. Everyone. The stories are usually interesting—and even if they aren't, you learn a lot about the person just by watching the manner in which they tell them.

It makes for good whiskey talk, and sometimes good pillow talk.

For some, it's beautiful. For others, it's a horror show. For me, it was, as the saying goes, "Tragedy + Time = Comedy."

Like all teenage boys, I had raging hormones. The vast majority of the conversations between my friends and me were centered on sex. Getting your hands on porn back in those days was work. Hard work. One friend's dad had a VHS of *Debbie Does Dallas*. Another guy had *Deep Throat*. We'd sometimes pay a homeless cat to buy us dirty magazines from the newsstand at the 'L' train station. Millennials and zoomers, be grateful for your internet porn. You have no idea how good you have it.

A couple of my friends had already had sex with their girlfriends, and the pressure was now on the rest of us. There was no way we were graduating high school without doing some sex, if we could help it.

I was developmentally a late bloomer, four-foot-eleven in my freshman year of high school and (thankfully) the six feet I am today by graduation. Suffice to say, I was not rushing 1,000 yards a game, nor banging the head cheerleader under the stands (but I'm pretty sure the guy who was had gone on to mow my parents' lawn). Generally speaking, it's best not to peak too early.

How was I going to make this happen? I'd always had a lot of female friends, but no prospects to speak of.

One night, I was out with a group of city friends. Downtowners. The cool kids with the lavish penthouses, brownstones, and absentee parents who, depending on heritage, were either investment bankers, commodities brokers, or descendants of slave traders. Out of nowhere, a new girl (who we'll call Leslie) approached me.

LESLIE: I hear you're a real sexual dynamo, Scott Nathan.

Was she flirting? Was she fucking with me? I'd basically never done anything with anyone. She wasn't particularly thin, or particularly attractive — definitely a strange bird, but no matter — but she had huge breasts. My chances, while remote, were all I had. *Let's see where this goes.*

ME: (Feigning confidence) Yeah… Well… you know … (Polishing my fingernails on my chest).

Previous to that night, she had been just a friend of friends. I got her number and we chatted on the phone for a week or so. How we arrived at this booty call, I have no recollection, probably because of the PTSD that followed it.

Seventeen years old. Chicago. A bitterly cold, subzero, snowy night. The brown-and-cream striped-cloth seats in my brown metallic '84 Toyota Land Cruiser wagon felt like cinder blocks. I used every bit of double clutching and manual gearbox skills to keep from becoming a fatality on the black-ice–covered roads that night.

I pulled into the valet at Leslie's father's luxury high-rise building on North Lake Shore Drive — terrified, thirsty, lump in throat, heart pounding. Not knowing what to do or say. The only breasts I'd touched up until this point belonged to my babysitter, Debbie, in fifth grade as a plea bargain to not tell my parents about her boyfriend coming over to visit.

The doorman took my keys and rang up. I arrived at a very dark, four-bedroom condo. The only light was a dimmed chrome Arco lamp hanging over a sectional sofa. She handed me a lukewarm bottle of Heineken and told me her father was in Miami for the week. It tasted bitter and skunked. For some reason, I was thirsty, but it seemed uncool to ask for water. We chatted awkwardly for maybe 30 minutes before she realized I was too much of a pussy to make a move. I was.

LESLIE: Have you ever driven a Ferrari?

ME: Been in one once, but haven't driven one.

LESLIE: Do you want to drive my dad's?

ME: Are you insane? It's an ice rink out there, and I barely made it here in a four-wheel-drive truck. Let's do it another time.

LESLIE: Fine. I'll drive. Let's go.

ME: OK.

So, 15-year-old Leslie and I headed down to the garage level and got in the car. A light metallic-blue Ferrari Mondial 8. Mid-engine. Tan, waxy, Connolly leather interior. No Ferrarista's wet dream, but pretty ace for two horny teenage kids.

We made it less than three blocks before she gunned the second to third gear change and 180'd the prancing stallion, wadding it up into bits against a North Lake Shore Drive street lamp, which showered me with passenger-side window glass. The glass was in my hair and down my shirt. It rang my bell. No major injuries, but my head and elbow hurt.

ME: You idiot. We're fucked!

LESLIE: We are NOT fucked. Let's go.

ME: We *ARE* fucked. You're 15. Where are we going?

LESLIE: Home to fuck. The car was stolen. That's the story. That's what happened.

It seemed so simple. Maybe she was right.

She was not right.

ME: OK.

We walked back across the tundra, up the elevator, and back to the apartment. I couldn't feel my face, hands, or feet. It was 20° below zero with an 80° below wind chill factor, and we were on Lake Michigan.

She put on the most popular record of the era, Pink Floyd's *The Wall* (vinyl, of course). As we were awkwardly getting naked, I was hearing the opening helicopters and the terrifying schoolmaster shouting,"YOU! YES, YOU!" This was not helping my opening-night jitters. At all.

I fumbled about with her nude, scratchy, front-opening, sensible, nylon bra, until she finally undid it.

LESLIE: You have a condom, yes?

Damn it. I knew I forgot something. Actually, it never crossed my mind. I'd never bought one before. Tunnel vision. Now panicking more than ever. She shook her head.

LESLIE: Just be careful.

ME: OK.

I was scared and visibly shaking, but I was going to get through this.

LESLIE: Be gentle, OK? I'm a virgin.

I was thinking, *Wait… what? You took the lead on this. You asked for the sex.* I was too proud and didn't divulge that I too was a virgin, and nodded.

We tried for a bit, and got it in. Barely. Nobody was really having any fun and we decided to call it quits. No orgasms. Not great. Fine. It was over. I wasn't a virgin anymore and I went home.

A couple of days later, something was terribly wrong downstairs. Walking down the hall at school, I felt something slippery down there. I hit the closest restroom to survey the situation. What the hell was this? It felt like sperm, but was yellow, like pee. Pretty sure I hadn't invented anything new. I gave it another day. It got worse.

Options were minimal.

If I told my parents, it would be unspeakably horrible and lead to conversations no one wants to have. Ever.

If I told my friends, I would never hear the end of the jokes about the fat girl and the VD. Neither STD nor STI were terms yet. I decided to go it alone to the local Planned Parenthood type place.

After a thorough examination, which included getting a thin, painful, metal wire with a tuft of cotton shoved into my urethra, I sat and I waited.

The nurse returned without the doctor. She was a heavyset black woman with a deep Southern dialect and a white, ribbed polyester zip-up jacket and matching white pants that made a *scraaaatchy* sound because her thighs rubbed together as she walked.

NURSE: Mmm, so baby… you've got the Gonococcus.

ME: Wait? What?

She was staring at me with a sad face, but said nothing.

ME: Is that like gonorrhea?

NURSE: Mmm, it *is* gonorrhea, baby.

ME: What? No, no. That's impossible. Are you sure?

NURSE: Mmm, yes, baby.

ME: Wait. But. No. No. No. She told me she was a virgin… Is it possible you mixed my test up with someone else's?

NURSE: (Making a sympathetic face) Mmm. Nooo, baby.

ME: Wait. She lied???

The nurse squinted and nodded yes, with a pained look at the naiveté on my face. Now it looked like she might cry. My lower lip quivered. My body convulsed. I felt as though I might vomit and shit myself at the same time.

I melted down on the spot and began to cry uncontrollably. She bear-hugged me and held up my limp body while I cried into the scratchy, ribbed, white polyester jacket for a good three minutes.

ME: Am I going to die? Will I have this forever?

NURSE: You ain't gon' die, baby. The doctor gonna give you some antibiotics. You'll be right as rain in a week.

She picked up a giant novelty brandy snifter filled with red, green, blue, and yellow condoms, and handed me a prescription for Tetracycline

ME: No, thank you. Not going near any women ever again. They're dirty liars.

NURSE: Take a few, baby.

I took the condoms out of politeness, but threw them into the parking-lot trash can outside. Later that day, I filled the prescription. The pharmacist's assistant was a girl in my car pool…

KELLY: Oh, no way! I take tetracycline too, but your skin is perfect!

(She thankfully hadn't noticed Planned Parenthood on the label.)

I had more than a few trust issues after that, and didn't speak to Leslie. Not even to tell her that she had given me the clap. Maybe I would've texted or emailed, but we didn't have such things then. I was so furious, and, I wasn't developmentally equipped to have that conversation.

I ran into her 10 years later, at a Mayor's black-tie event. As we were walking toward each other, we locked eyes and froze, like two bucks in the wild. She was approximately five-foot-three and 300 pounds. I was overjoyed at how porcine she looked.

She, of course, had got busted for destroying the Ferrari. The doorman had seen us on the security camera stealing the car and had told her father. An imperfect crime. She was sent away to boarding school.

"

A few months later she was found dead in a bathtub full of ice and frozen vegetables…

Chapter Three

Models, Heroin, Death, and the LAPD

2004

I was living in a nondescript, pink-stucco apartment building in Hollywood.

It was an eighties-modern but generic two-bedroom, two-bath place. During more prosperous times, I'd use the second room as an office or gear/guest room. When things got slow, I'd have roommates, usually friends, for between one month and a couple of years.

A few months went by and I couldn't find anyone I knew to move in, short or long term, when a modeling agent friend of mine suggested the agency rent the room from me for their "better" girls who wouldn't stay in the "models apartment."

"Models apartment." It sounded glamorous. Sexy, anyway. What an out-of-towner might think the Playboy Mansion would be like, but with better genetics and style.

The apartments were usually in decent buildings. Usually, three to four bedrooms, with sometimes three to four twin mattresses per bedroom on the floor. Overflowing ashtrays, burned and red-wine-stained carpeting, and rotting food. Kids running amok and no shortage of drama. "I know that bitch stole my underwear." "Someone left a used tampon on my bedspread." "Movie star X had sex with underage Mormon girl Y." And so on.

My rules were simple. No parties. No drugs. Don't be late on rent. Oh, and don't knock on my door if it's closed.

For a handful of years, it became a revolving door for a lot of friends I have to this day, and a lot of great memories.

This is not one of them.

I was introduced to a girl (we'll call "Stephanie") several years before. Everything about her was big. Built like a racing greyhound. An olive-skinned brunette, five-foot-eleven. Big eyes. Big smile. Big personality. And, from all reports, a big drug problem.

Her agent was a close friend, and came to me with the idea of her moving in. I expressed my concerns about the drugs, and she assured me Stephanie had been clean for ages.

I met with her, we talked, and decided to give it a go. She knew the stakes. If you fuck up, you're out, and I will dispassionately throw you and your shit into the street.

Everything was pretty smooth until month seven or so. The first sign of erratic behavior was her walking in on my girlfriend and me with the lights off, naked, and asking if she could sleep with us, because she had heard a noise and was afraid to be in her room. As you can imagine, my girlfriend was displeased with this idea, which turned into suspicion that something was going on between Stephanie and me. I assured her I wasn't a cheater and even if I were single, I would never get my tail where I get my mail.

We returned from a weekend at Korakia in Palm Springs, to discover a shopping cart full of things in the living room. Many of them, mine. The energy in the place felt black. Wrong. I opened her bathroom door and there it was…

Jackson Pollock meets Dexter. The Dark Side of the Spoon. A filthy, black, soot-covered, stainless-steel utensil; a few broken off, unused Camel cigarette filters; and a near-empty clear-blue lighter. I looked up to the cciling and there it was.

Horror. An expressionistic work made up of Squibb U-100 hypodermic needle squirts, containing a mixture of brown, dried blood and West Coast, Mexican black-tar heroin on the ceiling. Something I'd heard inmates on TV call "gravy." Sickening.

I ran to survey my bedroom. Yep. Camera cases gone. Two Leica bodies, two Mamiya RZ67 bodies, my Linhof 4x5 camera, a pile of lenses, my

'63 Stratocaster, and my Franck Muller watch. A first-gen Sony digital camcorder with homemade porn on it. All gone. My blood was boiling.

I called an emergency locksmith and had the locks changed. And I put what little she had into white-plastic garbage bags and placed them in the hallway.

She arrived back at the apartment and the drama began, right on schedule. LAPD was there. Banging on my metal door with a metal baton. They wanted to know why I had locked my roommate out and told me it was illegal to do so. I explained that I had no roommate. The lease was mine. She was briefly a guest and was a drug addict and a thief.

A new, 22-year-old neighbor guy who had just moved here from Alabama was charmed by her beauty, was sympathetic to her situation, and agreed to put her up. Poor hayseed bastard. She holed up in his place like a squatter and refused to come out. Welcome to Hollywood, kid.

There was a lot of yelling and histrionics in the hallway. After a while, I stuck my head out to see what was going on.

STEPHANIE: I have fucking rights! Don't come near me. I have Riiiiights!!!

I was wondering why the three cops looked so terrified of a scrawny, runway model. They were wearing blue nitrile gloves and were exercising extreme caution. Then I noticed it. Stephanie had forgotten to remove the syringe from the vein in her arm. It was just bouncing up and down in her arm as she was pacing, ranting, and raving. Blood was running down her forearm, and drip, drip, dripping from her fingertips onto the dove-gray hallway carpeting.

STEPHANIE: Don't you come *near* me! I have RIGHTS, you fuckers!

I went back inside and dead-bolted the door. She was removed and, thankfully, my life got quiet again. For five minutes, anyway. My girlfriend let me have it with both barrels for being too nice, too trusting, and too hopeful with broken people.

I never saw Stephanie again. A few months later she was found dead in a bathtub full of ice and frozen vegetables, left there by a guy who she was getting high with and who made almost no attempt to save her life.

But, as was the case with many junkies, his fear of getting busted outweighed any clear thinking or sense to call 911 from a pay phone.

I later found out who the guy was. Just a few weeks ago, I met him by chance at a store on my corner. He's a somewhat known actor and strangely, after 10 years, I felt no resentment toward him. He didn't kill her. Dope did. As Elvis Presley's friend Lamar Fike once said, "How do you save a man from himself?" Or as the Marines say, "Marines die. It's what we do." Same goes for junkies.

66

*As the area began to fill up,
I noticed that everyone else
in the waiting area was
a little person…*

Chapter Four

The Dwarf Audition

One of my dirty little secrets for the past dozen or so years is that, time permitting, I audition and occasionally work as a commercial actor. I've done around 40 spots over the years. I had fun and made good money. I consider myself to be a uniquely untalented actor. But in a narrow space (usually playing nerds) I can, on occasion, get a good joke or slice of improv off.

Given the fact that I mostly work as an advertising photographer and commercial director and the talent pool is so small, these auditions are rarely without an awkward exchange.

ACTORS & MODELS: Hey, Scott! You're directing this? I really hope we can work together.

ME: Hey, no. I'm auditioning.

They always look at me like I'm fucking with them until they realize I'm rattling a cup for change and health insurance just like they are.

One of the funnier auditions was a same-day casting email. It was for a Christmas-themed car commercial. I was driving, and quickly scanned the email for the time and the casting studio. I entered the studio and there was a sign that said "Volkswagen – Room 3." I signed in, grabbed a copy of the sides (show-folk speak for the script), and sat down to learn the lines.

As the area began to fill up, I noticed that everyone else in the waiting area was a little person. Dwarves. It's not that unusual for multiple categories to be going at the same time, so I ignored it and went back to the dialogue. I felt some stares but ignored them. Fuck 'em. Learn the shit. Book the job. Finally, I heard a woman's voice under her breath…

BIKER CHICK DWARF: Motherfucker…

I looked up and 10 or 12 little people were staring at me. The one vibing me was clearly the alpha. She had long hair, dyed black. Bitch bangs. Pale skin. She wore tiny, black-leather pants, a chain wallet, sleeve tattoos, motorcycle boots, a white tank top with a black bra underneath, and big breast implants. She was giving me the death stare. Unafraid, I looked her square in the eyes and shook my head.

ME: Uh… problem?

BIKER CHICK DWARF: (Shaking her head, muttering) Oh fuck you.

Then one of the little guys walked over to me. He seemed alright.

LITTLE GUY: Hey, man. Sorry about my friend. I know you don't mean anything, but Christmas spots are the one time of the year that all of us little guys get to work, and ever since mother fucking *Lord of the Rings*, they've been taking people your size and CG'ing them down.

I didn't know what to say….

ME: Hey. My agent told me to be here, so I'm here. I went in, did the audition. Felt OK.

Cut to 8 p.m. My phone rings.

AGENT: Hey. Asshole. When you confirm an audition, I expect you to be there and not embarrass me.

ME: I was there! Volkswagen. Did they say I didn't go?

AGENT: Volkswagen? This was for Hyundai.

ME: Fuck. I was wondering why I was the only person that wasn't a dwarf.

We started laughing hysterically. Next day:

AGENT: You have a callback for Volkswagen.

And, scene…

"

*I was afraid to lie to the cop,
and given that he was obviously
a Second Amendment advocate,
I decided to fess up.*

Chapter Five

Guns, Marijuana, and the Texas State Police

I was visiting a friend at his ranch in a town called Independence, Texas, between Houston and Austin. There wasn't much around his place other than a Walmart, a Chili's, and a gun shop. I decided to borrow his Suburban and head to Austin.

Texas roads are long, flat, and remote. I was cruising along at around 90 MPH when I got tagged by a Texas State Trooper.

TROOPER: License and registration, please.

ME: Yes sir, officer. Here's my license. This is my friend's truck. Mind if I look around for the registration?

TROOPER: Go ahead. California, huh?

It's no mystery that Texas cops hate California and Californians like Hamas hates Jews. OK, maybe not that much, but it certainly wasn't helping the proceedings.

ME: Yes, sir.

I didn't see the registration in the glove box and had just peeked into the center console to notice my buddy's loaded .357 Magnum.

I quickly closed it before the cop saw it *(hopefully)*.

TROOPER: I don't understand you people in California *at all*.

In a vain attempt to connect with him, I took a swing.

ME: What's to understand? We all want the same things. Be happy. All that. No?

TROOPER: I don't understand a state where you can smoke all the marijuana you want, but you don't have a right to defend yourself or your family.

ME: Officer, I can't say I disagree with you there. I've been an NRA life member since I was 13 years old.

Anecdotally, I had sternly resigned that membership years ago, due to their extremist politics and Russian money laundering.

TROOPER: Do you have any drugs or weapons in the vehicle?

Then I got nervous. I was afraid to lie to the cop, and given that he was obviously a Second Amendment advocate, I decided to fess up.

ME: Definitely no drugs, but I did notice that there's a loaded .357 Magnum in the center console. Belongs to my friend, who must've left it in there.

TROOPER: May I see it, please?

ME: (Opening the center console and pointing) Sure.

TROOPER: Would you please pick up the pistol and hand it to me?

ME: I'd really rather not. Do you mind if I just hop out and you grab it?

TROOPER. Do not exit the vehicle. Hand me the pistol, please.

ME: Where I grew up, cops who kill people ask them to pick up their gun and hand it to them first.

TROOPER: (Laughing) Why would I kill you?

ME: Yeah, but I don't know you…

I couldn't have been less comfortable, but… no choice.

ME: OK, so I'm picking it up with two fingers… by the muzzle… and handing it to you… OK?

TROOPER: (Rolling his eyes) Colt Python. You've got some fancy friends.

ME: Yeah. Very nice.

TROOPER: How much ammunition do you have?

ME: I think just what's in the gun.

TROOPER: (Smiling) Traveling a little light aren't you, California? (Handing me my license) Slow down and drive safe.

"

His was one of the all-time great WTF faces I've ever seen. His eyes darted around the room until he caught my wave…

Chapter Six

The Wedding Shoes

May, 2012, Los Angeles, California

I had just wrapped a meeting where I learned I was awarded the job to shoot some print ads and billboards for the California Milk Advisory Board. It was a new installment for the iconic series "Happy Cows Come from California." As always, I was excited to work, but also to spend a few days working with animals and their wranglers at Sony Pictures.

This was a job where I had to share the day with the crew shooting the commercial. Typically, the stills photographers are treated like second-class citizens, but this wasn't unit or BTS photography — it was for billboards and print ads, and I needed to get good shots.

As I left the meeting, the producer said, "You'll be working with Fred Savage."

ME: *The Wonder Years* Fred Savage?

PRODUCER: Yes.

ME: I didn't know he still acted.

PRODUCER: He's directing it. He's a big commercial director and directs for *Modern Family*.

ME: Cool.

At wrap, I took the obligatory photo with Fred Savage and posted it on Instagram.

On my way home, I got a call from Jason Biggs.

JB: Hey pal. Looking at your Insta. Are you with Savage now?

ME: We just wrapped three days. Headed home from set.

JB: If you talk to him, would you please tell him to pick up his wife's wedding shoes from my house?

ME: Why are his wife's wedding shoes at your house?

JB: This used to be their house and they left them behind. We've tried to get other people to let him know, but never heard back.

ME: He's married with kids and lives in The Valley. I doubt I'll ever see him again, but if I do, I'll tell him.

A few days later, I was having lunch in the garden at Soho House.

I looked up from my meeting and saw Savage sitting at a round six top. He was gesticulating, apparently pitching something to a group of suits.

I texted Biggs.

ME: (Jokingly) Hey. I'm at lunch and Savage is here. Do me a favor, get your dick hard, put it in his wife's wedding shoe, and take a picture. I'll text it to him in the middle of his meeting.

One minute later, Jason sent the photo of his dick in the tiny satin wedding shoe. Either that or Jason has a really big penis. (I'm working off the small-shoe theory.) This is one of the many things I love about Jason. He will do *anything* for a laugh. The mark of a true comic actor.

I looked up Fred's cell number off the call sheet on my phone and texted him the photo. It took a good two minutes until he picked up the phone, looked confused by the number not in his contacts, and opened the message.

TEXT: This is from Biggs asking for you to pick up your wife's wedding shoes.

His was one of the all-time great WTF faces I've ever seen.

His eyes darted around the room until he caught my wave from a few tables away. He wasn't smiling at first. After his meeting, he walked over with a big grin on his face, put a hand on my back, and leaned in.

SAVAGE: We're never picking up the shoes. Jason and Jenny trying to get them back to us has become my favorite game.

"

"I drink too much, but at least I'm not smoking crack anymore. That's kind of what led to my divorce."

Chapter Seven

Malibu Anal Barbie

Spring, 2012

I received a friend request on Facebook from a cute blonde living on the beach in Malibu. We had a good number of friends in common — mostly musicians and other photographers. I accepted.

We began chatting. Not flirting, just joking around. She told me she just wrapped up her divorce from an older guy who made a fortune selling some kind of health or fitness snake oil on infomercials. He had bought her a pied-à-terre on the water in a gated community.

She was funny. Physically, a Pamela Anderson type, blonde hair with long (but good) hair extensions. A lithe, size zero body with massive breast implants. She had four Old English Sheepdogs.

I'm rarely one to make the first move. After a few weeks of this, I waited for the invitation, until:

BARBIE: You should come out and visit. This beach is a nice place to wake up.

Doesn't get much clearer than that. The foundation had been poured. This was mine to lose.

I set out around noon in my 12-year-old black Mercedes. Not wanting to appear too presumptuous, I didn't pack an overnight bag, just a little backpack with the basics: bottle of water, two T-shirts, underwear, toothbrush, small bottle of sunscreen, three condoms, and some silicone-based lube just in case.

I rang the bell, then heard the dogs barking and her cute, scratchy voice.

BARBIE: One sec!

She opened the door. She was cuter in real life. She was wearing an oversized white tee, no bra, and cutoffs. Tanned and barefoot. She invited me to sit down. She was loaded on something, but I couldn't tell what yet.

BARBIE: If you want to charge your phone, you can plug it into that iMac.

ME: I'm good. I'm charged from the drive out.

BARBIE: Actually, don't plug it into that one. I have it set up to rape phones.

ME: What?

BARBIE: Yeah. I have this software. People plug their phones in and I steal their contacts, photos, and videos. I wouldn't do that to you, though.

Cue red flag number one.

ME: Hmm.

She grabbed a plastic 1.75 liter handle of Sauza Silver off the table and took four massive, air-bubbling slugs, like it was ice water after a run. Christ.

ME: Is it happy hour already?

BARBIE: I drink too much, but at least I'm not smoking crack anymore. That's kind of what led to my divorce.

Here we go… I nodded, said nothing, and let her talk. And talk. When someone wants to confess, stay out of their way.

After a while she told me she was going to take a bath. Cool by me. We were on her deck at a long wooden dining table overlooking the ocean. It was hot and sunny. I had the dogs around me. *I'm good.*

After 30 minutes or so, I went inside and discovered the whole house was flooded out with water and a foot of soap bubbles. WTF? Did she drown in the tub? I ran into the bathroom and shut off the faucet of the large, overflowing white Kohler tub.

I walked into her bedroom and she was folding laundry. The bedroom was also flooded.

ME: Hey! Your tub is overflowing!

BARBIE: Oh, I alllllways do that… It's like being in heaven. The bubbles are like clouds…

She kicked a merengue-like bubble cloud floating down the marble hallway.

Here we go.

I took the bottle of Sauza and stashed it under the kitchen sink. The bar was closed. She'd had enough for one afternoon.

She took a long bath, while I sat between the two sinks talking to her and keeping her company. She got out and I handed her a white hotel robe. We sat on her bed and talked for a while, then watched a mindless action movie on Netflix until we both fell asleep for a few hours. I made no moves. I didn't even think about it. There was nothing sexy about this situation, and she was in no condition to consent.

I should mention that her bedroom was literally that. A few hundred square feet of mattresses. Multiple kings and smaller sizes to fill in gaps with white linens, a lot of Moroccan pillows. It was really cool and I guess good for someone with a lot of dogs (or orgies).

I woke up and it was dark. She was wrestling with my belt.

ME: Um hey…

BARBIE: Do you want a blowie?

It'd been a few hours. She was sober enough to know what she was doing.

ME: Yes.

Five minutes into it, her phone rang and she took a call with her girlfriend on speaker.

FRIEND: Is he there?

BARBIE: Yes.

FRIEND: Is he cool? Are you OK?

BARBIE: He's great. I'm sucking his cock right now.

FRIEND: OK, I'll let you get back to it.

HER: No, that's OK, tell me what you've been up to.

They talked for another 10 minutes. She successfully alternated between talking, sucking, and jerking. It was quite an impressive juggling act. I videoed the whole thing.

She got off the call, then put her phone in selfie video mode and made a video of the blowjob. I went with it.

BARBIE: Take your pants off and fuck me.

ME: I love a romantic.

I obliged. About 15 minutes passed.

BARBIE: Put it in my ass…

ME: No way. You're not prepped. I don't do unplanned anal.

BARBIE: (Belligerent) You think I'd ask you for anal if it wasn't a good time? Anal is my thing. It's the only thing that makes me cum. Now shut up and stick your cock in my ass.

ME: Yes, ma'am.

I obliged again, slowly. About three minutes in, she had a fulminating blowout. From the top of my abs to the middle of my thighs I was covered in thick, viscous shit. It was a stink for the ages.

We all accept a certain amount of risk while playing the back nine, but this was a lot. I recoiled in horror, leapt from the giant bed, held my breath, and made a run for the bathroom.

In all of this shock and awe, I had forgotten about the flood earlier. It was too late. I slid on the soap-and-water-covered travertine floor. Both feet shot straight up into the air and I landed smack on my tailbone. I screamed. I was writhing in pain. My back was covered in cold, slimy water and my front covered in feces. I needed to get through this now and be in pain after. I reached for the edge of the tub to slowly pull myself upright. This was the kind of pain that would last for five days.

Wincing, I tiptoed an inch at a time into the shower only to discover there was no more hot water. I took an icy shower, breathing through my mouth while scrubbing the shit from my body.

Shivering, in agony, but now clean, I walked back to her doorway. She was snoring, her white bedding covered in shit. The next decision was easy — get the fuck out. I crushed a Norco 10/325 between my molars and chased it down with a warm, bedside bottle of Fiji. I then quietly put on my clothes and grabbed my backpack. As stealthily as possible, I slipped out the front door. It was a cold, moonless night. I had wet hair. I was shaking and couldn't wait to get in the car and get the seat heaters on.

As I was walking to the car, I fumbled my keys and they hit the ground, splitting the computerized key down the middle. *Fuck. What do I do? Go back into her place and risk waking her up? NEVER.* I called AAA and waited 40 minutes. They said it would be no more than 30. Frustrated, I called them back. They told me the guard wouldn't let them through the gate without Barbie's go ahead.

I began walking to the gate, teeth chattering. I explained to the guard that she was passed out and we'd be out in 10 minutes. He relented without much argument. I hopped in the tow truck cab with the driver and pointed the heat vents on my body. As he was filling out the paperwork, he looked up at me.

TOW TRUCK DRIVER: So, with your Auto Club Plan, it's going to cost $350 to get your car back to Hollywood.

ME: No no. I have the Platinum package. 100 miles. I've gotten my bike towed back from Santa Barbara.

TOW TRUCK DRIVER: You have 100 miles for motorcycle, 10 for car.

ME: Forget it. I'm not paying $350.

TOW TRUCK DRIVER: Are you sure?

ME: Yes, go!

I don't know what I was thinking in this blind rage, but he was now gone. I took a beat and decide I was going to fix this broken key. I had no tools to speak of. I went through the detritus in my trunk and found a roll of gaffers tape. *Patiently*, I began to experiment with thin strips of tape and the filaments. I examined the key and decided that if I tightly wrapped both plastic key body parts around the printed circuit board and battery, it should make contact well enough to start the car.

It didn't. Not at first. I was squeezing the now sticky body of the key and shoving the key in and out of the ignition. In nothing. Out nothing. Frustrated, I picked up pace, subtly changing the pressure.

After 10 minutes or so — DING! I turned the key, started the car, and prayed it didn't kill the ignition while driving. It didn't. I made it home. The next morning, I remembered I had already lost the other key a year earlier. I dug up the plastic card with the code on it and called Beverly Hills Mercedes Benz. They let me know the cost of the key was $300. Resigned, I stayed calm, sucked it up, and jumped in an Uber to pick the key up at the parts department counter.

I was at Santa Monica and Doheny in front of the Troubadour when my phone rang. It was Barbie.

BARBIE: Hey baby! Where are you?

ME: Hey. I'm in West Hollywood.

BARBIE: I had the best time with you yesterday!

ME: Did you? Because it was one of the worst nights ever for me.

BARBIE: Why do you say that?

ME: Barbie! You shit all over me.

BARBIE: Well, that's what you *get* for fucking an alcoholic in the ass.

She had a point.

We had a series of long talks about her addiction issues, ending with her accepting that it was time to get help. She said she didn't have enough money to go to rehab, but agreed to go if I could find her a free one.

I was owed a favor from another woman, a former model named Jaime. I had helped her get sober a dozen years earlier. She had been working in the rehab business for years. She wasn't able to find Barbie a bed in rehab without cost, but after a few Skype calls, we managed to get her cast onto one of the rehab reality shows on cable for a season. It worked.

Barbie and I still chat a few times a year. She moved back to New England and bought a house near her parents. She's managed to stay sober ever since.

"

*Law of the universe.
If you don't give a shit, it
will come to you as sure as
the sun will rise.*

Chapter Eight

Alcohol, Tobacco, and Scientology

2005

I never had dreams of being an actor when I moved here. I didn't generally like actors. For one, I'm mostly an introvert. Second, I never wanted to be anything where the occupation could also be used as the insult. Example: "Shut up, you fucking actor."

Anyway, I met this woman at a party who seemed to think I was "geek chic" and could make some money *and* health insurance as a commercial actor. I was reluctant, but as it turned out, she was right. I made piles of money and had a lot of fun. Law of the universe. If you don't give a shit, it will come to you as sure as the sun will rise.

Loathe as I am to admit it, I met some great people. Many of them actors. Many of them now close friends. Here's an excerpt from our first meeting:

AGENT: So, is there anything that you won't advertise for?

ME: I'm not sure I understand the question.

AGENT: Some people won't advertise for certain products they're fundamentally opposed to.

ME: Like what?

AGENT: Fast food?

ME: No problem.

AGENT: Tobacco?

ME: Fine.

AGENT: Liquor?

ME: I love liquor.

AGENT: Scientology propaganda films?

ME: You're kidding, right?

AGENT: No. They make all kinds of short films and they pay great. Since you're so skinny, you'd be a great drug addict for Narconon.[1] We respect all actors here and would never ask you to do anything you're uncomfortable with.

ME: Listen. I'm Jewish and if it pays SAG scale, I'll do infomercials for the Nazi Party.[2]

AGENT: Perfect. Welcome aboard.

---

1 Narconon is the drug rehabilitation arm of Scientology.

2 I already see this line as a pull-quote in a review. It's a joke, people.

"

I couldn't outfight them. I couldn't ignore them. I couldn't really out-anything them, so I decided to play the crazy card.

Chapter Nine

Won't You Be My Neighbor

Chicago, Winter of 1992

I had just moved into a new loft. Three-thousand square feet with city views and a freight elevator that could get my Harley up to my apartment. It was in a terrible neighborhood, near the corner of Sangamon and Lake, but the place was so cool and I was in my early 20s. You know, that age where you're positive you know better than everyone else? I didn't just carry a gun to and from my car. I carried it in my hand.

Anyway, this gangster rap group (but really just gangsters) had moved in below me. Back in those days, it was not easy to stay up partying later than me. Bars closed at 4 a.m., 5 a.m. on Saturdays, and I was out 300+ nights per year. My old oak floors were their ceiling and you could see into their unit through the gaps in the floorboards. I put up with a few days of their after-hours partying and shitty music before I lost my temper. To say I was drunk was an understatement. It was Chicago. An average night out was nine cocktails. In '92, my drink was Absolut Citron rocks with lemon and I drank rivers of it.

I jumped up and down on my floor as hard as I could, dropping massive amounts of dust into their unit and probably knocking things off shelves.

ME: SHUT THE FUCK UP! SHUT THE FUCK UP! SHUT THE FUCK UP!

This didn't go over very well with the gang members. A minute later, they were banging on my door. I looked through the peephole and there were three of them. Two of them holding 40s of OE8.

In situations like this, you're either a lion or an impala. Growing up a skinny redhead, you learn these lessons early. They were neighbors and weren't going anywhere, so I had to handle this. I couldn't outfight them. I couldn't ignore them. I couldn't really out-anything them, so I decided to play the crazy card.

I pulled a gleaming six-inch nickel-plated Colt Python .357 Magnum from my desk drawer. It was my most cinematic pistol. My dad used to take me to see all the *Dirty Harry* movies, and it felt like the right choice.

I was as white as paper, had flaming red hair past the bottom of my rib cage, and stood six feet tall at 118 pounds. Like Jesus (only armed and drunk). I was wearing white, Brooks Brothers Oxford cloth boxer shorts and nothing else.

They continued to pound on the door. Very quietly, I unlocked the deadbolt and walked backward 20 feet from the door.

ME: (In a high-pitched, musical register) COME INNNNNNN!!!!

They opened the door and saw me standing with the pistol at my side. Smiling my biggest craziest smile, cocking my head left and right.

With a big, toothy grin, I said…

ME: SUP, FELLAS? ANYTHING I CAN DO FOR YA?

The third guy in the hallway muttered:

GUY 3: This mufucka crazy. Let's bounce.

And bounce they did. I'd see them in the freight elevator from time to time. I'd say hi. They'd look at the floor.

Let me be clear. I do *not* recommend this technique, but it worked this particular time.

"

*So, we walked back to
my place and did some sex.
Face-meltingly fun.*

Chapter Ten

The Whore Wisperer

A handful of years ago, I was shooting a hair campaign for a startup brand out of Orange County.

The setup was fairly standard. Four or five models of various hair colors and ethnicities. Shooting a variety of looks with a lighting setup of my choosing on a white, gray, or black background. Bread and butter. Nothing fancy. Something I'd done hundreds of times before.

My longtime assistant Stewart and I have systems in place. Our own language, workflow, and so on. Jagger/Richards, Lennon/McCartney, only far less talented.

I had gotten through two models. Every angle. Every option.

ME: OK. Bring out the next one.

STEW: Uh dude. She won't come out of the closet.

I looked up.

ME: Huh?

STEW: She's locked herself in the janitor's closet and won't come out. I think she's crying.

ME: Huh? Why?

Stew shrugged.

ME: Take me to the closet. What's her name?

STEW: Annie.

ME: (Upbeat tone and three gentle raps on the door) Annie! It's Scott. The photographer! It's show time!

ANNIE: (Wailing) You can't come in!

ME: Annie! The show must go on.

ANNIE: OK. You can come in, but no one else!

I walked into the closet and sat down next to her. She was wearing nothing but a nude thong. Her mascara was everywhere. It was all over her face and had run down her breasts. She was wailing.

ME: Annie. What happened?

ANNIE: That motherfucker cut off all of my hair and called me a cunt.

ME: Wait. What? Who?

ANNIE: The d-bag.

ME: Which d-bag?

ANNIE: That old loser with the tribal tattoos, Range Rover, and spray tan.

She had just described the whole of male Orange County, but I knew who she meant.

ME: The client?

Great… Now I was furious. No one talks to anyone on my set like that, especially a young girl. I don't care who it is. I was thinking how to handle this when I realized being a new client, I required payment in full in advance. The impulsive redhead emerged as I walked up to him.

ME: (Snaps fingers and points) HEY. Did you cut all my model's hair off without permission from her or her agency and then call her a cunt?

D-BAG: Yeah. I'm paying that cunt for 10 hours and I'll do whatever the fuck I want to her.

ME: (Enraged, to my assistant) Pack up the truck. We're out of here.

D-BAG: Leave and I'll sue you.

ME: Fuck you. You have no idea how vindictive I can be. I'll put her on TV and destroy you and your brand with a wave of my hand.

Mexican standoff.

Now I was thinking about this, I knew I didn't need a lawsuit. Nobody wins them except lawyers. I took a deep breath.

ME: I'll finish the job conditionally, and it's not negotiable. You pay Annie in full *now*, and you let her go home. If the check bounces, you will never see the files from this shoot.

D-BAG: Fine.

Cut to three days later. Annie called to thank me. I said no thanks necessary—that guy is a fucking tool and I'll never work for him again.

She asked if she could take me to lunch. I told l her it's totally unnecessary and sorry she went through that. She persisted and we went to lunch at the place on my corner.

We'd been talking for 90 minutes or so about where we're from and what we do, when, out of nowhere, she asked:

ANNIE: Hey. Do you wanna have sex?

ME: (Eyes widening) Uh. Yeah.

So, we walked back to my place and did some sex. Face-meltingly fun. That continued about quarterly for the next few years. She was impossible to ever reach and I stopped trying. I'd hear from her whenever I'd hear from her. We'd have the occasional slumber party. She traveled a lot to exotic places, but I assumed it was for work. Not sure which kind.

Most recently, I got the call and she asked if she could come over for sex and maybe spend the night. Of course. Always a good time. Never any complication. Just five feet ten inches of poreless, perfect, 23-year-old magnificence.

So again, we did the sex that afternoon, again at night, and again in the morning. After morning, she said she was going to take a shower. Ten minutes later I felt the phone vibrating in the sheets and began fishing around for it.

I found it and noticed a banner that said, "Annie. You have a notification from Mohammed at Seeking.com." Having no emotional investment in a woman too young to be my daughter, I laughed and shouted:

ME: Hey, babe?

ANNIE: Yeah, babe?

ME: (Holding back laughter) Mohammed from Seeking Arrangement is trying to reach you.

ANNIE: Oh my God! Are you spying on me? Why are you looking at my phone?!

ME: I thought it was mine. Why on earth would you have notifications turned on?

At this point, I decided to act super into it so I could gather more information about this. I smiled mischievously.

ME: Show me your hustle. Show me how it works.

Her big green eyes lit up and a big grin washed across her face.

ANNIE: OK. You wanna see my hustle? Watch this!

She dialed and on speaker phone we heard Mohammed, with a strong Middle Eastern accent.

MOHAMMED: I'm at the Peninsula in Beverly Hills. I would like to take you to lunch.

ANNIE: It's a thousand to take me to lunch. Venmo it to me now or I'm hanging up.

MOHAMMED: OK. I send you now.

True to his word, the money came seconds later.

ANNIE: Can we go shopping after lunch?

MOHAMMED: Yes, of course.

ANNIE: Hey. So I'm going to go to lunch and shopping, but I'm not fucking this guy. I fuck maybe three percent of these guys, but they're guys I would fuck anyway, so... Can I come back in three or four hours and we'll play some more?

ME: Sure.

True to her word, at 3:30 sharp, she was back. Shopping bags in hand. A massive Saint Laurent shopping bag containing high boots, two handbags, and a pair of heels. In her other hand was a smaller bag from Gucci, which she handed me.

ME: What's this?

ANNIE: I got you a present!

I opened the bag and shoe box and there was a pair of horrendous velvet slippers with fur on them.

ME: That was very nice of you. Two questions. How did you convince Mohammed to buy you a pair of men's shoes, and how did you know I was a size 11?

ANNIE: I told him it was my dad's birthday and I didn't have any money. I got your size out of your closet.

ME: (Laughing) You're amazing. So, are you making a lot of money from these dates?

ANNIE: That's the problem. I'm rich in designer stuff, but I never have any money.

ME: Well, let's fix that. First things first: Only have them take you shopping at Barneys or Neiman Marcus from now on.

ANNIE: Why is that?

ME: Those are two stores that I know of that will give you actual cash instead of a store credit on a return.

ANNIE: OK. I'll try it.

A month or so went by before I heard from Annie again. When I did, she was very excited.

ANNIE: Daddy, you're a genius!

ME: Hey! Why am I a genius?

ANNIE: Remember when you told me to only shop at Barneys and Neiman's with sugar daddies?

ME: Oh! Yes.

ANNIE: Well, I've been doing that and I now have over $31,000 in my bank account. You're so smart, Daddy. You should be a consultant for Instagram models! You're like a whore whisperer!

"

*The ONE time you go to the
mailbox in your underwear
drunk in the middle of
the night…*

Chapter Eleven

Kate Moss and the Elevator

Los Angeles, 1996

I arrived home from a hard night of after-hours drinking at the Sunset Marquis. I was as white as snow (with boiled-ham pink accents) and my hair was down to the bottom of my rib cage. At six feet tall, I weighed maybe 130 pounds soaking wet.

I took off my clothes and realized I forgotten to check my mail for money I badly needed. There weren't security cameras in my building yet, and my Macallan whisky–soaked brain told me, "Just jump in the elevator in your underwear. There's no chance you'll see anyone at 4:30 a.m. It's only two floors."

As luck would have it, the doors sprang open and who's standing there?

ME: Fuck! I am so sorry!

Kate's eyes squinted shut. Disgusted, she let out a barely audible "Ugh." In a vain attempt to un-freak her out, I attempted a joke.

ME: Y'know, the ONE time you go to the mailbox in your underwear drunk in the middle of the night, of *course* Kate Moss is standing there.

Kate looked down at her shoes, eyes still clenched shut.

ME: Floor?

KATE: (Sighing) Fourth please.

Kate turned and faced the wall.

*Bear Spray 1, Dickhead 0.
I tried posting this as an
Amazon product review of
BearGuard, but it was rejected.*

Chapter Twelve

Boobs, Bear Spray, and Road Rage

A round 1996 I got invited to the Playmate of the Year party at the
newly opened Sky Bar at the Mondrian Hotel on Sunset Boulevard.
There were a lot of orange-hued, short girls with single-process blonde
hair, cheap, bolt-on boobs, and a lot of cocaine. I never liked cocaine,
but there weren't many motorcycles, golf courses, or boobs I didn't like,
so I figured I'd have a look around and drink some free booze.

I ended up in a suite belonging to Vivid Video CEO Steve Hirsch and
met this cute, smart, charming actress. We were both wearing all white.
She was blacker than volcanic glass, I was pinker than a Christmas ham,
and we were both amused by the contrast. We were also both bored by
the performative, and terribly unsexy lesbian threesome going on in the
bed in front of us.

We became fast friends and would have the occasional slumber party to
pass the time between relationships.

It was a rainy night and I was driving east on Wilshire Boulevard
through Koreatown, en route to her place in this old hotel called the
Gaylord. It was across the street from the Ambassador Hotel, where
Robert F. Kennedy was assassinated, and above this dodgy, Bukowskian,
pre-hipster, nautical-themed bar called the HMS Bounty.

I was chatting on the phone to a friend to pass the time, when I heard
a horn honking. Not a "clearing of the throat" beep beep honk, but a
constant, rage-filled one. Like 15 straight seconds.

I realized that I had ever so slightly drifted into this guy's lane and quickly moved back into my own. No brakes were slammed. No big deal.

We got to the next light and he was still honking his horn. He was in a big metallic-gray Dodge RAM pickup truck. I rolled down my window.

ME: Hey. Really sorry about that.

HIM: Get off the fucking phone, asshole!

ME: Yeah. Totally my fault. Again. Sorry.

HIM: Pull over!

ME: I said I was sorry.

HIM: I said, pull the fuck over! I want to talk to you.

ME: Hey. I apologized. I said I'm sorry, but there's no way I'm pulling over.

Guy floored it through the red light and curbed me by diagonally blocking my car.

Guy went crazy. Jumped out of his truck. He slammed his fists on the hood of my old black '87 Saab 900 Turbo. He then came around to my side. He began kicking my door in and pounding on my driver's window screaming. The glass was flexing and I was sure it was about to shatter.

This was not good.

Years before, at the suggestion of my friend's frightening Israeli psychiatrist father, I bought some grizzly bear pepper spray called BearGuard. Since it was illegal to carry a gun in your car in Chicago (and California), it seemed like a decent, legal way to protect oneself in the car.

I reached into the door pocket for this huge can that resembled a mini fire extinguisher and pulled the orange pin on it.

I rolled down my window about three inches, just enough to get the nozzle clear. I pulled the trigger on the can, and a cloud of this stuff covered the guy from his abdomen to his forehead. From the sounds that followed, it may as well have been a flamethrower.

He hit the ground bellowing. My heart was beating fast and I was scared, but I couldn't help but be amazed at how awesome this stuff was.

As he lay flat on his back on the rain and oil-soaked boulevard, I could see from the streetlamp light that his face was redder than an orangutan's ass. His eyes were swollen shut. He looked like Sylvester Stallone at the end of the first *Rocky* movie. There was a whitish foam coming from his nose and mouth and he was howling in agony.

HIM: I'm blind! You fucking blinded me.

ME: (Proud) Yeah, asshole! Anyone else would've shot you. What have we learned about getting out of cars and attacking people? What have we *learned*, asshole?

HIM: (Rolling around, crying, writhing in agony) Fuck you! You blinded me!

Boiling over with adrenaline, I wanted to get out of the car and kick his nuts in, but decided to avoid escalating the issue. I didn't call 911. I didn't tell the girl.

On my way home in the morning, his truck was still there. It had parking three tickets on it. Bear Spray 1, Dickhead 0.

I tried posting this as an Amazon product review of BearGuard, but it was rejected.

"

I was standing, burning in the sun, handcuffed on graduation day wearing a black satin polyester graduation gown.

Chapter Thirteen

College Graduation Night

Recently, I was talking with some old friends and I asked them what they had done on grad night. Almost none of them could seem to remember exactly how they had spent it. "Dinner with my parents." "A keg somewhere, maybe?" "An 8 ball of cocaine and a nitrous tank?"

I remember mine. That's for certain.

Immediately after commencement, my parents had a flight to catch out of Stapleton Airport in Denver, about an hour from the University of Colorado at Boulder's campus.

We piled into my 1984 Camaro Z-28, red with silver side skirts, and I dropped them off. It was a growling, vulgar, fast, and garish American muscle car of no particular historical significance, but it was mine, and at the time I thought it was cool.

In a hurry to get back to the parties around campus, I burned up those Goodyear Eagle GTs and hightailed it back across the then mostly desolate front range of the Colorado Rockies between Denver and Boulder. I was still in my gown.

Nearly halfway back, I saw Mars Lights in my rearview mirror. *Fuck!* Colorado State Police. They were everything you'd expect: Ridiculous miniature cowboy hats, bolo ties, and mustaches—pagan, dog-fucking, lifer assholes.

Speaking of assholes, I was an out-of-state, spoiled college asshole with a new car, Illinois tags, long hair, and a Grateful Dead "Steal Your Face" sticker between the rear glass and brake lamp. T-top's off, wearing a graduation gown, and clocking 94 MPH. In hindsight, I'm not sure who was less likable at a glance, but at the time I was sure it wasn't me.

TROOPER: License and registration.

ME: Yes sir, officer.

TROOPER: Do you know why we pulled you over today?

ME: Yes, sir. I was speeding.

Twenty minutes of silence went by with them in their cruiser.

Since my 16th birthday, I had accumulated literally dozens of speeding, reckless driving, and even one "fleeing and eluding the police in a high-speed chase" tickets (but I'll save that story for another time). If history had taught me anything, it was that everyone lies to the cops and they really hate it. My olive branch was to eat shit, take the ticket, and get on my way.

In the pre-Greylord trials era in Chicago, breaking almost any law was a simple inconvenience. It involved either paying off the cop on the scene with a $100 bill paper-clipped to your driver's license or dropping off an envelope full of cash bearing the name of a particular dead person at a particular room number at the La Salle Street courthouse, which would then be divided among the prosecutors, judges, and God knows who else.

It was a great system, but I knew better than to try this maneuver on a couple of Bible-thumping shitkickers in Colorado.

The troopers reappeared on either side of my car.

TROOPER: Mr. Nathan, we're gonna need you to step out of the car with your hands on your head.

ME: Wait. What?

TROOPER: You've got a warrant out for your arrest and we're placing you into custody.

ME: That's impossible. For what?

TROOPER: Step out of the car now or I'll add resisting arrest.

ME: OK! OK! Can you please tell me what the warrant is for?

They handcuffed me and refused to answer me for nearly 40 minutes.

I was standing, burning in the sun, handcuffed on graduation day wearing a black satin polyester graduation gown. I was fucking livid.

ME: Hey! Are you going to tell me why I'm being arrested?

TROOPER: You have an FTA Warrant.

ME: What's an FTA?

TROOPER: A Failure to Appear in Court.

ME: No. I don't. For what?

He walked away. Another 20 minutes dragged by…

The trooper cited a statute number.

ME: You'll forgive me, but I don't have your code book memorized. You wanna tell me what it is?

TROOPER: A bicycle ticket for a crosswalk against a don't walk sign.

By now, my patience had admittedly worn thin.

ME: You have *got* to be SHITTING ME. You're handcuffing me and possibly arresting me, on my graduation day, for a *bicycle ticket*? Can't I just pay the ticket here and now?

TROOPER: We're definitely arresting you. Are you attempting to offer us a bribe?

ME: What? Oh, my God. No!

TROOPER: Since you're graduating, we're going to assume you'll leave the state without paying this.

ME: I promise I will pay it. (More silence) Fine. Where's the closest police station? Let's just get this over with.

They towed my car away and took me to a crossroads between wheat fields in the middle of nowhere. They wouldn't answer any of my questions, my fuse was lit, and my respect for these dickless idiots was over.

ME: Why the hell are we just sitting here? It's my graduation night! Do you think this is the best use of state resources?

This was followed by more asshole dialogue from me and more asshole behavior from them.

Finally, in the distance a white school bus appeared. Flat white, like it was brush painted. Diesel exhaust stains. Steel mesh, like the pattern you see on wrought-iron patio furniture, crudely welded over the windows. Stenciled in black on the side: "Adams County Department of Corrections."

ME: Would you please explain to me what the hell is going on here?

TROOPER: There are no police stations nearby, and you're going to Brighton.

ME: Brighton, the prison? Is this a fucking joke? You're going to put me in Brighton? For a bicycle ticket?

No response from Barney Fife or his partner who looked like his mother had eaten lead-based paint chips while he was in utero.

Trooper #2 opened the car door, put his hand on my head, and took me out of the squad car.

ME: You aren't seriously going to put me on a bus full of fucking felons wearing a graduation gown. At least let me take it off!

Trooper #1 unlocked a single handcuff, put one wrist in front of me and one behind me, and re-cuffed me so not only could I not walk upright, but there was no way I could possibly remove the gown.

The bus full of felons was really just four other guys who didn't say anything. We pulled up to Brighton, which had high fences topped with coils of hurricane razor wire, and it was pretty terrifying.

We went through multiple steel doors and checkpoints. Cops checked their weapons. The smell was dank. The fluorescent light was green, paint on the walls was thickly layered and yellowed, and the linoleum floors were old with foot-traffic holes worn through to the concrete.

The sounds were foreign and unsettling. Walkie-talkie static and chirps, loud buzzes from security doors opening and closing, and cell doors slamming. This place sucked.

TROOPER: We've got a treat for y'all tonight. College boy here thinks he's better than everyone else.

ME: I do NOT think I'm better than everyone else. I just think I'm better than YOU.

I didn't shut up for the next hour, which didn't help and I knew it wouldn't, but I was already fucked and had no patience in those days.

I was handcuffed to a steel eye bolt on a concrete bench. More time went by. Fingerprinting, mug shots, idiotic questions about aliases, tattoos, scars, and other nonsense, most of which were met by sarcastic and fake answers.

They started moving me toward a holding cell containing two enormous, prison-tattooed black guys. Especially terrifying was the fact they were smiling.

ME: (To guard) Hey, I want my own cell. If anything happens to me, do you have any idea what's going to happen to you?

(Yes, I realize I'm an unsympathetic character at this point in my life. I was a giant, mouthy pussy from the suburbs who wore cricket sweaters and white pants. Let me be clear about that.)

They guided me into the cell.

ME: Hey, guys.

INMATE #1: (Laughing at my graduation gown) What's up, Judge?

INMATE #2: (Hissing with laughter) Ss-sss-sss-sss-ss.

ME: Judge? What? Oh yeah. My gown. Real funny. (Yelling out to guards) Hey! When do I get my phone call! (No response) HEY!!!

My fellow inmates turned out to be pretty cool guys (as far as armed robbers go). Thirteen more hours went by before I got to make my phone call. This was long before there were any cell phones or pagers. School was already out and most people had shut off their utilities for the school year. I figured the Fraternity House was my best bet. Nope. Disconnected. I didn't want to call my parents, since they were not only back in Chicago, but couldn't help anyway.

Bail stipulations were that someone I knew had to bring physical cash in person and give me a ride home. I couldn't think of anyone else who still had a live phone line.

ME: I need another phone call. Line was disconnected.

GUARD: Go ahead. One more.

I decided on a wildcard idea and called the Boulder Limousine Service.

I'd used them a lot for airport runs over the years and knew the owner pretty well. I also knew their number by heart, which was essential.

A recording played as the owner answered.

"This is a call from the Adam's County Department of Corrections."

LARRY: Boulder Limousine.

ME: Larry? It's Scott Nathan.

LARRY: Scott?

ME: Yeah. Hey, I need a huge favor. Huge.

LARRY: Yeah? Wassup?

ME: Do you still have my Amex on file?

LARRY: Yes, sir.

ME: I need you to do a charge on my card, get cash, pick me up from jail and get me out of here.

There was a bit of back and forth. Larry was worried about doing something wrong. I assured him it was OK and he was my only shot. He agreed. We hung up.

GUARD: We monitor calls, and there ain't no WAY we're allowing that!

ME: You said I needed cash, a ride, and someone I know. I've satisfied those three things and you have no choice but to let me out of here!

GUARD: You can't call a limousine company.

ME: The hell I can't. The guy is my friend!

We argued for the next 10 minutes.

A meeting of the halfwits commenced between three of them and they said nothing to me. I saw in the small, black-and-white, Motorola CRT security monitor, Larry's old beat-up, silver Lincoln stretch had arrived. The high fences were closing behind him.

They decided to let Larry post the bail.

GUARD: Nathan. You made bail. You're free to go.

ME: Yeah, I know. I hope you get in a disfiguring car wreck. I hope develop a slow and painful stomach cancer. Seriously. Fuck all of you.

I walked back through the labyrinth of steel doors out onto the asphalt lot. It was cold and the sun was rising. I got in the car.

LARRY: Yo, Scott. (Handing me a glass) Stoli Rocks?

ME: Fuck, yes. Thanks, Larry. I owe you one.

*She was a vaudeville dancer,
pals with the Three Stooges, and
by far, my blondest, tannest,
most glamorous relative.*

Chapter Fourteen

The Secret to Outliving Everyone You've Ever Known

Spring, 2007

I was in Palm Springs for a weekend (as I am wont to do) and decided to visit with my Great-Aunt Ide. She was, give or take, 100 years old and on her deathbed. Given that the vast majority of our family is east of the Mississippi, I visited her when I could. Not so much out of obligation, but because she was a great storyteller and supremely funny. She'd only given up driving a few years earlier.

Previous to buying her house off South Palm Canyon Drive for $25,000, she had lived in Laurel Canyon when it was still primarily a mountain lion hunting community. She was a vaudeville dancer, pals with the Three Stooges (who, evidently, were avid opium enthusiasts), and was by far, my blondest, tannest, and most glamorous relative. She was known by me and my cousins simply as "Aunt Ide from California."

She told me tales of sex with Isaac Stern and her outspoken opinions of Bob Hope when we'd see him at Canyon Country Club.

Her lovely Filipino nurse had just made us some really average tuna fish sandwiches on white bread, with iceberg lettuce (the polyester of the garden) and left us to visit in her room.

Perhaps 15 minutes had gone by without anyone saying anything. As many of you know, I don't have much of a filter and blurted out the following.

ME: So, you've outlived everyone you've ever known?

IDE: (With a grin, her blue eyes twinkling) Every last one of 'em.

ME: Is it lonely?

IDE: No, dear. It's the best.

ME: What's the secret?

IDE: Do you really want to know or are you just uncomfortable sitting here quietly with me?

ME: I really want to know.

IDE: Life's a very simple game, made complicated by us. I never worried about a goddamned thing in my entire life. My friends who worried the most died first. My friends who worried the least died last. And I worried less than them. I win.

ME: You've never worried?

IDE: Not during the Great Depression, not after the death of my husband. Not ever. I knew that everything would always work out, because it always does. I smoked, I drank, I stayed out late. I had fun.

ME: That's it?

IDE: Yes. You know, dear… more than one person called me a whore in my life.

Yeesh.

ME: I'm going to get something to drink. Do you want anything from the kitchen?

"

She took a sip of champagne and shifted position again, revealing former President Bill Clinton.

Chapter Fifteen

Bill Clinton, the Model, and the Dalai Lama

To say that I have an interesting group of friends is like saying Antonio Stradivari made a half-decent fiddle. I have this model friend. Super sweet and down to earth. REI type from NorCal.

She was dating this new guy but wasn't ready to tell me who he was yet. All I knew was that she was living a lavish lifestyle and she's not the escort type.

Anyway, she FaceTimed me from her iPad aboard what was obviously a private jet. She was giggling, visibly buzzed, and holding a half full champagne flute.

I've seen a few jet interiors in my day. This one was different.

ME: Holy shit. What kind of plane is that? It's massive!

ERICA: Do you want me to find out?

ME: Yeah, if you can!

ERICA: (Walking with iPad to the flight deck, then knocking on the door) HEY GUYS! What kind of plane is this? My friend likes planes and wants to know.

CAPTAIN: (Waving to me) It's a Boeing 757-200.

ME: Thanks!

She was walking back to her seat. Earbuds in.

ME: Good plane. You going to tell me who he is yet?

ERICA: Not yet. I will if it ends up being something.

She was sitting in a lush cream, high-back leather seat. Shifting positions, I noticed the unmistakable view of His Holiness, the Dalai Lama in saffron robes over her left shoulder.

ME: Dude. Is that the Dalai Lama behind you?!

ERICA: Yes! Do you know him?

ME: No, I don't *know* him!

ERICA: He's super nice!

ME: He's like the 14th reincarnation of Buddha. I'd imagine the very *least* he would be is nice.

ERICA: (No idea what I'm talking about) What?

ME: Nothing.

She took a sip of champagne and shifted position again, revealing former President Bill Clinton.

ME: Dude, is that Bill Clinton talking to the Dalai Lama?

ERICA: Yes! Do you know him?

ME: No, I don't know him either!

ERICA: He's really nice! Do you want to meet them?

ME: Yes!

She walked over to them.

ERICA: HEY GUYS, MY GOOD FRIEND SCOTT WANTS TO MEET YOU!

She got on one knee between the two of them, holding the iPad in her outstretched arm, selfie style. I suddenly processed the fact that I was in bed and shirtless, making this even weirder. I didn't know what to say and it was too late.

They were waving and smiling.

BILL CLINTON: How ya doin', bud?

DALAI LAMA: (Smiling and waving) Helloooo.

ME: (Ambien waving) Mr. President. Your Holiness.

She was walking back to her seat.

ME: Dude. Where are you going with *them*?

ERICA: Monaco!

ME: What are you doing in Monaco with Bill Clinton and the Dalai Lama?

ERICA: Partying! Duh.

The following day, she texts me a photo of a bottle of wine on a table.

ERICA: I just had the best wine. Literally LOL.

Not being an oenophile, I decided to text the photo to someone I know who is—Robert Mondavi's grandson.

ME: Any good?

CARLO: Cannes?

ME: Nope.

CARLO: Nice?

ME: Nope

CARLO: Monaco?

ME: Yes.

CARLO: That is literally the fakest '47 Chateau Cheval Blanc I've ever seen!

ME: Are you sure?

CARLO: One hundred percent. Bottle is wrong. Label is wrong. Cork is wrong. Let me guess. Some billionaire bought it at a restaurant to show off?

ME: Yep.

CARLO: Was probably good wine in the fake. Probably another high-end, first-growth Bordeaux, but another sucker scammed.

"

"Ken Paves spent hours putting in the most beautiful hair extensions and now she's cutting them all out with toenail scissors!"

Chapter Sixteen

Britney Spears 2007 VMAs

September 9, 2007, late afternoon

I was sitting in bed about to take a nap when my phone rang. It was my friend Celia. (I have permission from my friend, but changed her name anyway.) We've known each other for many years. We only end up seeing each other a couple times a year, but it's always fun and hilarious.

Celia is a diminutive blonde from New England. She's sexy, charming, and somehow always has had so many interesting jobs, I've never been able to keep track of them.

The phone rang out of the blue.

ME: Hey!

CELIA: Scott Nathan, I need your help! (She always calls me by my full name.)

I quickly sat up.

ME: What do you need?

CELIA: I'm backstage and Britney won't put her costume on... WAIT. *Hang on, Scott!* Britney! You need to put your costume on. You CANNOT go onstage in your underwear!

ME: Britney who? Where are you?

CELIA: Spears!

OK. Celia has another crazy gig and this time, it's babysitting Britney Spears.

BRITNEY: (In background) But I don't wannnnna put it onnnnn and YOU don't get to tell ME what to do…

ME: Where *are* you?

CELIA: We're backstage at the VMAs! She has to go onstage NOW!!! Oh my God, Scott! Ken Paves spent hours putting in the most beautiful hair extensions and now she's cutting them all out with toenail scissors!

I really didn't see how I could be of any help, so I turned my TV on and watched this fiery train wreck burn in real time. Celia was fired on the spot. Britney had security kick her out of the backstage area. Celia went back to her suite at the Palms, ordered a pitcher of martinis, and proceeded to cry and drink away her sorrows.

A short while later, there was an incessant knocking at the door of her Suite. She looked out the peephole. It was Britney Spears. Alone. Celia opened the door.

CELIA: What do you want?

BRITNEY: Let's go out clubbing!

CELIA: No! You fired me!

There was a lot of back and forth. Britney didn't want to talk about what happened earlier, nor did she like being told no. And that, as they say in France… was that.

"

What's the worst thing you've ever done to another human being?

Chapter Seventeen

My Shortest First Date

Summer, 2016

I was getting a morning coffee at this place up the street in Hollywood. As I was waking up and checking my phone, an attractive blonde in a vintage Army shirt and denim skirt complimented my boots.

We began chatting. I noticed her Australian accent. She'd been in LA for three years. She seemed intelligent, nice, and well put together, and she knew how to use a curling iron.

We chatted for another half hour or so and as I stood, she said, "Let me give you my number." I told her I'd call her later on.

We decided to meet for dinner that night. I ordered a glass of wine. She immediately looked panic stricken, ordered nothing and told me she was newly sober.

ME: Ah. I see. What was your substance of choice?

Whether someone is a junkie, a drunk, a speed freak, or a coke head, if you're paying attention, it will tell you almost everything you need to know about their personality type.

RACHEL: Everything.

That's no help, I thought.

RACHEL: Listen. Scott. I've done some things I'm not proud of.

ME: Well, so have I. Who hasn't?

RACHEL: No. I mean, *really* not proud of.

I paused, looked her in the eye, and asked.

ME: What's the worst thing you've ever done to another human being?

RACHEL: I was getting high with this 18-year-old girl and she OD'd. And while I felt bad about putting her out in the alley and not calling 911, for whatever reason, I felt much worse that her parents probably thought she died alone, shooting heroin in an alley in Hollywood.

ME: I like to think that I am, generally speaking, without judgment, but... I'm going to go.

RACHEL: (Looking unsurprised) K.

"

Then she grabbed a giant fistful of Splenda packets and shoved them into her purse. I was aghast.

Chapter Eighteen

My Second Shortest First Date

Two weeks ago, a college pal from Boulder called to check in. He has a new girlfriend and wanted me to come by and meet her.

ME: Happy for you. What does she do?

DAVE: She's a therapist and a rabbi. You'll love her.

ME: She's not going to like me.

DAVE: Yes she will. She's not what you think.

ME: I'm a foul-mouthed sinner who eats pork and shellfish.

DAVE: It'll be fine. I promise.

I went to the house in the foothills of Studio City. She welcomed me in, and I instantly felt a sense of *haimishness* from her. Haimish is a great Yiddish word for warm and unpretentious. I liked her from the first moment. Dave was still getting ready. We sat down and she mentioned she had seen some of my TikToks. I was expecting someone extremely *frum* (observant.) In my experience, I've found orthodoxy in any religion to be uptight, humorless and not taking kindly to my type.

I was wrong this time.

ME: Oh dear. Apologies in advance.

RABBI: I thought they were very funny and entertaining. Your shortest first date was rather shocking.

ME: Yes. A lot of the stories are bad dates. I try to find a way to laugh at trauma.

RABBI: What was your second shortest date?

ME: Not quite as dramatic. We met at the Coffee Bean and Tea Leaf at the corner of Sunset and Fairfax. It's a Starbucks now, (but what isn't?). We chatted in line and she seemed nice enough. Then, as we were gathering our napkins and stir sticks, she grabbed a giant fistful of Splenda packets and shoved them into her purse. I was aghast.

ME: What're you doing?

DATE: What? They're free.

ME: They're not *free*. They're to use while you're here. Not to stock your house with. Jesus Christ.

DATE: (Rolling her eyes) I think you have anger management issues.

ME: I think you're the reason the world is shittier than it has to be. Selfish behavior from people like you leads to anarchy. I'm out.

I gave a shrug to the rabbi.

ME: So that's the story.

RABBI: Do you realize that you exhibited textbook Talmudic, Rabbinical wisdom?

ME: What?

RABBI: In the story of Noah's Ark, what provoked God to carry out the most serious environmental catastrophe in human history, wiping out all terrestrial creatures, traces back to petty dishonesty. That the greatest risk to humanity is not those who are intent on destroying it, but rather the collective unintentional actions of billions of people committing seemingly benign crimes… People in Noah's generation went to the open market and stole a peanut here. A raisin there. With no one being tried or punished for these minuscule crimes, the store owners over time all had to shut down. In retaliation, God flooded the earth, wiping out almost everyone.

“

I put my hands in my pockets.
I'll play a round of golf with
a pariah, but I'm not shaking
his hand.

Chapter Nineteen

Golf with O.J. Simpson

Late 1995, Encino, California

My friend and fellow Chicago native Bob and I decided to play golf at a San Fernando Valley Park District course called Encino/Balboa. We paid our fees, collected our cart, and headed to the first tee.

On the tee was a mid-30s and very fit African American cat in running gear. Royal-blue Nike tank top and matching short running shorts— and a black, sun-faded, generic lightweight carry bag. We introduced ourselves and shook hands.

ME: Is there a fourth or are they just sending us out as a threesome?

RUNNING GUY: I'm a single.

ME: OK, let's tee it and if someone gets here before we take off they can join us. Otherwise, we'll go out as a three.

Bob and Running Guy nodded in agreement. As I was pulling a worn Titleist Tour Balata 100 and a blonde long tee from my pocket, I saw a guy approaching us. I elbowed Bob.

ME: (Whispering) Hey! (Followed by a nod)

It was O.J. Simpson, whom, nearly a year earlier, was exiled from LA's fabled Riviera Country Club before his murder trial ever began. (Evidently he wasn't really The Riv's look anymore.) He was just recently acquitted in the criminal trial, but hadn't yet started the civil trial.

As he walked up, I noticed he was presenting more like he belonged at his former $300,000+ country club than at this muni dog track we were playing. Perfect, snow-white and brown, leather-soled FootJoy saddle shoes; tailored, tan trousers; a matching cashmere sweater vest; white polo; and a khaki unbranded visor.

BOB: (Whispering) Nathan. There is no fucking way I'm playing with that murderer.

ME: (Whispering) Oh, *yes* you are.

BOB: (Still whispering) No fucking way.

ME: Fine, then take a cab home. I drove, and I want the story.

BOB: Fuck you.

O.J: (All smiles, loud and enthusiastic) Hey, fellas! How you doing?!

No one said shit at first. I put my hands in my pockets. I'll play a round of golf with a pariah, but I'm not shaking his hand.

ME: Oh. Hey.

O.J: (To Running Guy) How you doin', brother?

Running Guy refused to make eye contact. He looked pissed and quietly muttered while rifling through his bag.

RUNNING GUY: I'm not *your* brother, motherfucker.

O.J. went from all smiles to super scary. He was *pissed*.

O.J: (Booming) SAY WHAT?

Running Guy stood and took three giant strides toward O.J., then leaned in, nose to nose with him.

RUNNING GUY: I SAID… I'M NOT… YOUR BROTHER… MOTHERFUCKER.

Things are what you might call awkward at this point.

O.J. picked up his tour-sized, yellow and white vinyl Cleveland Golf bag. The kind of golf bag that you could fit a Catholic family into. The kind of golf bag only touring pros and other guys who never have to pick one up would own. His name was embroidered in shiny black thread.

O.J. picked up the bag and started to walk away. Except, when he got maybe 40 feet away, he 180'ed on his heels, slammed his bag down, and shot Running Guy a physically aggressive look. He looked ready to fight.

Running Guy put his arms out like Jesus (only palms up), his eyes widened, and he quickly slapped both of his pectoral muscles *hard*, outstretched his arms again, and looked O.J. squarely in the eyes.

RUNNING GUY: S'UP??

O.J., knowing his bluff had been called, walked away fuming.

RUNNING GUY: (Muttering to no one in particular) Fuck that motherfucker.

Our first few holes were pretty quiet. No one brought him up for the rest of the round. We saw him here and there on neighboring fairways playing with another group.

"

"Are you a crazy person?…
Are you willing to risk everything
on someone who isn't a model and
has never modeled for anything?"

Chapter Twenty

My Single Dumbest/Smartest Career Move

In 2005, after a lifetime of passionate enthusiasm, I began my professional photography career. I was encouraged by a friend who was a veteran pro himself.

I began as a digital tech, possibly the first one in the business. Pro digital cameras were still an emerging technology and given that I was an IT consultant at places like Universal Pictures and The Walt Disney Company, I was suited to learn the workflow.

The deal I made with my friend was that I would work on set with him and run the cameras and the computers. In the process, I'd learn to navigate the waters of commercial celebrity and fashion photography as well as advanced studio lighting.

About six months into the job, one of the executives from Smashbox Cosmetics, with whom I had worked on set numerous times, pulled me aside and asked if I was capable of doing similar types of images to what we had been doing with my friend at the helm.

I said yes, and she asked if I'd be willing to put together a creative brief for a baby brand called Too Faced Cosmetics. I was familiar with them to the extent that they had always used cutesy stock illustration, and never photography. She admitted that she was overseeing change and looking to grow the brand up a bit. I accepted the challenge and put together my brief.

Now, mind you, beauty was nothing I ever set out to do. It was something my friend did, but wasn't particularly interesting to me. I wanted comedy, color, irony. Big, fun stories. That said, you take what you can get and I didn't even have a portfolio to speak of at the time.

The brief played off the name "Too Faced." Two faced. Two models. One good girl. One bad girl. Yin/Yang. One blonde. One brunette. More or less like every James Bond film, Archie comic, or episode of *Gilligan's Island.*

I asked for two casting days.

Casting day one was blondes. I saw approximately 125 models that day. When Lyndall Jarvis walked through the door, I knew she was my girl. Icy blonde, exotic, sapphire eyes, bee-stung lips. A South African with an inaccessible and intimidating presence.

Day two was brunettes. I saw maybe 100 and didn't remember a single one. I just wasn't feeling anyone. I needed another casting day.

ME: (To client) I didn't find our girl. I need another casting day.

Client: You saw 100 models in LA and you can't find a single brunette that will work for our brand?

ME: Nope. This is important. One more day. Please?

CLIENT: Fine.

I saw another couple dozen girls the following day. Now I was nervous. I called the CEO.

ME: Listen. There's no one here. Can we look at girls in New York?

CLIENT: Scott. No! We don't have the budget to fly and house New York models.

ME: I have an idea. I have this friend of mine I want you to meet.

CLIENT: Which agency is she with?

ME: She doesn't have an agency. She's not a model. She's not tall enough to be a model and she's not thin enough to be a model, but I think she's going to be a big star.

CLIENT: Actress?

ME: No. Singer.

CLIENT: That's an interesting idea. What label is she signed to?

ME: She doesn't have a record deal.

CEO: Are you a crazy person? Do you really want to put your balls on the chopping block on your first campaign? Are you willing to risk everything on someone who isn't a model and has never modeled for anything?

ME: Yes.

CLIENT: What's her name?

ME: Katy Perry. Will you meet with her?

CLIENT: (Nervous) Sure. Bring her in. But if I don't like her, I'm picking someone from the tape.

ME: Fine.

Later that night on phone:

ME: Perry.

KATY: Hey, Nathan.

ME: I'm picking you up at 11 a.m.

KATY: For what? I'm writing with Glen Ballard tomorrow who I've been stalking for months.

ME: Reschedule it. Look fun and festive. Trust me on this one. It'll be fun and there's money involved.

KATY: OK. I trust you and God knows I need money. See you then.

As anticipated, Katy managed to charm the pants off everyone in the room. We listened to her demo CD and took a spin through her MySpace profile and the two of us sold it in the room.

Didn't turn out half bad. The pink ballerina costume was something Katy had already owned. I had art department make up some wallpaper to match the color and pattern of the costume, and rented the famous Brigitte Bardot bed from a prop house.

Shoot highlight:

The CEO was a poncy gay cat with diamond rings on every finger, a Birkin bag, bleached blonde hair and orangey liquid foundation.

Trying his best to help, he said…

CEO: OK! So, Katy. Just relax and be yourself. I want you to do whatever you'd be doing at home in bed right now.

KATY: OH! OK!

She arched her hips high in the air and shoved her hand into her panties.

The CEO ran away shrieking. Katy looked over and gave me a wink.

After a bit more struggle, things ultimately worked out for Katy. My campaign was a hit and I went on to shoot four years and 16 seasons for Too Faced. That led to landing The Sephora Book of Beauty, Urban Decay Cosmetics (which got me fired from Too Faced), and dozens of other beauty brands and ultimately to that becoming my specialty.

66

*We took turns hitting the ball
and shooting it with the shotgun.
One of the best games ever.*

Chapter Twenty-One

Kidnapped by Hunter S. Thompson

Summer of '87ish, Aspen

I was a student at the University of Colorado at Boulder and had taken a liking to spending summers there. Boulder is just better than Chicago in the summertime. My parents had come to visit for a few days and I met them in Aspen for a getaway.

We stayed at the Hotel Jerome, a historic Victorian hotel that sits on the corner of Main and Mill in the center of Aspen. It's just below Red Mountain and across the way from Aspen Mountain, locally referred to as "Ajax." Four stars, but in that possibly haunted, *Butch Cassidy* kind of way. It was the best hotel at the time before the luxury chains moved in. The few times I stayed there, I had always requested a particular standard room just over the front door. It was the only room with a terrace I could smoke on, and it had a great view of the mountain.

My parents and I were getting on each other's nerves, as is typical for an early 20-something going through a lot of change and experimentation. Eh, who am I kidding? We still get on each other's nerves.

We had gotten into it pretty good and I sought refuge at the hotel bar. It was nice and quiet in the afternoon as I sipped glass after glass of Macallan 12 on ice.

Ninety minutes or so in, the room changed. Two loud, high-fiving frat boy dickheads in shorts and pastel tank tops had taken notice of another patron at the other end of the bar. One Hunter S. Thompson.

I had recognized him an hour earlier as I'd seen him speak at a campus event at Chautauqua Park at the base of the Flatirons in Boulder. I just didn't care. His heyday was a bit before my time, but he always struck me as a poser. A bullshit artist. I respected his hustle. I loved his articles, but only *liked* his books. I know this will piss some people off, and that's alright. As Henry Ford said, "There's an ass for every seat."

What struck me as strange was that he wasn't bothered by these moron fans. He seemed to bask in their attention, something that made me respect him a bit less.

The word fan itself was introduced into English around 1550 and means "one who is marked by excessive enthusiasm and often intense uncritical devotion." I got more drunk and less patient. They got louder and more irritating as Thompson told barely coherent, drunken rambling stories. Finally, I'd had enough.

ME: (Glaring) AY! Would you shut the fuck up down there? You are so full of shit!

Everyone got quiet. Looking straight ahead, I took another sip and realized Thompson was standing right next to me. Smiling. Signature long-billed baseball cap. Weird, Hawaiian type of shirt. Nut-hugger shorts.

HST: Yeah, but don't tell those knuckleheads.

He was smiling and amused by my shit attitude. I looked him in the eyes. Just taking him in. He smelled like cigarettes, blended whiskey, and day-old sweat.

HST: Do you like guns?

ME: No. (Long pause) I love them.

HST: Do you play golf?

ME: Yeah.

HST: Let's get out of here.

I was four or five whiskeys in and wanted to see where this went. Hunter settled his bill and the bartender placed a silver Taittinger champagne bucket full of ice on the bar. Hunter carried it outside like it was a normal thing to do. We walked to his car, an immense land yacht. The ice bucket was between us, and a bottle of Chivas Regal was unsheathed from a brown paper bag and jammed into the ice.

Hammered, we headed at high speed out of town. Past McLain Flats Road and out toward the airport. We were leaving Aspen. Where were we going?

We ended up at his house in Woody Creek, a town I hadn't previously been to. It was dated, rustic but cool. Stone fireplace. A taxidermied owl. bric-a-brac everywhere. We chatted a while. It didn't take long, but I liked the guy. He was funny. Much of our banter felt like well-rehearsed, time-tested one liners. I didn't hold it against him. It's kind of my move too.

One moment of note was our mutual love of English motorcycles. Him: BSA. Me: Norton. I hadn't yet owned a Norton, but my father had a couple of them new, and it wouldn't be long before I'd own my first. Dad called his Commandos "the one ways," meaning he could ride them as far and as hard as he wanted. The moment he turned around to come home, it would break down and Mom would have to pick him up.

Somewhere along the way he handed me a drink of some sort, a concoction that looked and tasted like bitter Hawaiian Punch. I figured it was Campari, or Pimm's or something. An old person aperitif.

ME: You said something about guns. What have you got?

He waved to follow him. We were outside. There was an old barn and a cliff.

He came out with an old shotgun. Nothing fancy. A working man's pump gun. A farm gun. An old Winchester with a corncob forend like the cops used to have mounted in their front seats. I expected him to have something cooler. Maybe an old Parker side by side with Damascus barrels. In his other hand, he had a copper Ping 9 iron. I told him I was left handed and couldn't use it. He shook me off. I decided to swing lefty, toe down. It worked alright.

This game had a name, but that name escapes me. I wasn't feeling well at all. Dizzy and nauseous. I can't remember if I'd had anything to eat. Whatever the case, I powered through and we took turns hitting the ball and shooting it with the shotgun. One of the best games ever. Respect Now I really didn't feel well. I turned and threw up a few times in the scrub.

ME: Hey, Hunter. I'm not feeling well. Can you run me back to the hotel? I drank too much and am really dizzy.

HST: (Muttering) Eh, no big deal. Just a little mescaline. No big deal.

ME: You dosed me with Mescaline?

HST: Uh, yeah. You're welcome.

ME: Mother. Fucker. Fuck. You! No! I have an eight p.m. dinner with my parents!

HST: Yeah, you're not going to make that or anything else for at least the next 8 to 12 hours.

He continued to hit balls off the cliff. There were no cell phones or pagers in those days and I thought it best to call my parents before the sky caught fire.

ME: Hey, Mom. Listen, I ran into a friend and I think I'm going to stay here tonight.

MOM: (Furious, in her shrill, nasal Chicago accent) What the hell are you talking about? Get back here! We're only here for a couple days!

Not knowing what to do, I hung up.

The rest of the evening is a bit hazy. People came and went. His girlfriend was kind. I stared at that owl on the shelf a lot. Someone gave me a ride back around sunrise.

66

Whenever I'd see him, he'd only stand or pace. I'd always offer a chair and he'd say, "Nope. You can't die standing up."

Chapter Twenty-Two

My Great-Uncle Jake

January 10, 2014

My great-uncle Jake passed away today at the ripe age of 98. Hilarious guy. Retired young and spent most of his adult life traveling the world sport fishing and playing poker.

Whenever I'd see him, he'd only stand or pace. I'd always offer a chair and he'd say, "Nope. You can't die standing up."

A couple of years ago, I went to visit him in Palm Springs. Knocked on his door, and he opened it looking frantic in his white Bermuda shorts, pale yellow cashmere V-neck with a white polo underneath.

JAKE: Scott, I've got big problems. You've gotta help me!

ME: Oh, no. What's wrong?

JAKE: You know that sexy nurse that works here at the house?

ME: Yeah, Janet, right?

JAKE: Right. Anyway, she hasn't gotten her period in three weeks and I don't know what I'm going to do.

ME: Oh, my God. Really?

JAKE: No, not *really*. I'm 96. Want a drink?

Godspeed, Uncle Jake. Hell of a run. See you on the other side.

"

The mushrooms kicked in hard.
I narrowed my gaze at this
one cage with almost no wait…
for 100 MPH fastballs.

Chapter Twenty-Three

Sports and Psychedelics

Summer of '84

Two of my childhood friends, Mark and Eli, were looking for something to do on a hot, sticky Chicago night. We decided to each take an eighth of liberty caps and go to the batting cages. We were quickly disappointed to learn that it was over an hour wait for every cage... except one.

We bought a plastic pitcher of Old Style with our fake IDs and sat at a picnic table covered in cracked green paint.

The mushrooms kicked in hard. It was that moment where the pressure in your skull is released, but just before the explosive laughter. I narrowed my gaze at this one cage with almost no wait and watched one person after another attempt, and fail, at the 100 MPH fastballs. I looked at the guys.

ME: I can hit the hundred.

ELI: Dude. If you go into that cage, you're GOING to DIE.

ME: Guys, I'm telling you, I can see it in slow motion. I can count all 108 red laces on that ball.

ELI: Please don't go in there. I really don't want to be tripping in an emergency room.

I was doubtless. I went to the counter and bought three 25-ball tokens. I missed the first ball entirely, chipped the second, then proceeded to pound the next 73 clean like I was peak, steroid Barry Bonds. That feeling where it doesn't even hurt your hands. Where you hit it so pure, it just goes "click."

I could hear the murmurs behind me as the crowd grew. By the end, roars and applause.

At the end of 75, I had proven my point. I was sweating and tired, and my hands were chewed up from batting without gloves. I put the bat down and my friends were screaming, laughing, and bug eyed.

A group of people followed us to the parking lot.

BIG CONTRACTOR GUY: (*Heavy* Chicago dialect) Hey, guy! You're awesome! You should join our city softball team.

ME: Hey thanks, but nah.

BIG CONTRACTOR GUY: C'mon, guy. Gimme your number! You're one of the best hitters I've ever seen.

ME: Thank you... but I don't really play well in groups.

66

Squinting, I noticed that all of the women were either not wearing pants or had their dresses hiked up.

Chapter Twenty-Four

Orgasmic Meditation

Summer of '84

An actress friend of mine asked if I wanted to join her at her meditation class. Sure. I'm on board. I like classes in just about anything. Gives me something to do. I once even took a cheese class when I was lactose intolerant.

She referred to it as her "OM" meditation class, which I presumed was the vibrational mantra one performs at the beginning and end of a yoga class.

Turns out I was wrong. "OM" in this case is O.M., an acronym for "Orgasmic Meditation."

She instructed me to meet her at 8:30 p.m. but no earlier. Had she just told me the time, I would have arrived as instructed. Actually, I'm never late and probably would've still arrived 10 or 15 minutes early.

The space on North Fairfax Avenue was a storefront. The windows were blacked out with duvetyne. I was surveying the space and noticed a small gap in the drapery. I peeked in, and at first glance it appeared to look like a yoga studio, which was what I was expecting. On closer inspection, I saw there were two-person teams, like what I would expect a Lamaze class to look like.

Squinting, I noticed that all of the women were either not wearing pants or had their dresses hiked up. Their legs were splayed open, like when you dissect a frog in high school biology class. The soles of their feet touched, and the men over them were wearing a single latex glove and touching their vaginas with a single outstretched index finger.

My phone rang. It was Sophia, the actress that introduced me to this actress. She's Latin, Catholic, and conservative.

SOPHIA: Hey. What're you up to?

ME: Hey, I'm about to walk into Salma's[1] meditation class. Do you know anything about her... practice?

SOPHIA: She's kind of a hippie. I'm sure it will be nice.

ME: Um, I'm looking through the window and these women are all naked from the waist down and appear to be getting finger blasted by men.

SOPHIA: Scott Nathan, what the hell are you talking about?

ME: I'm telling you. This is what I'm seeing with my own two eyes.

SOPHIA: That is DISGUSTING! What kind of sick, degenerate thing is this?

ME: I'll let you know...

The clock struck 8:30. The door unlocked and a few people walked out to the sidewalk. Out walked Salma looking.... dewy.

SALMA: I'm so glad you made it. Come in. I'll introduce you to everyone.

She made some introductions and asked me to help her assemble some folding chairs into a circle like I was at an AA meeting.

The room smelled like a sex shop. Latex, water-based lube, and (sorry) pussy. Fifteen or so people formed a circle. Most were there before I arrived. A few were newcomers like me. The women were mostly in their 40s and 50s. The men were awkward 20- and 30-somethings. A strange, rather horsey-looking blonde woman was staring at me intensely. I looked up a couple of times and finally gave her a pleasant smile back.

I won't go into a lot of detail about the practice, but it's basically edge play. The men, collectively referred to as "the strokers," are taught to, with the tip of their index finger, gently rub the upper left-hand quadrant of the woman's clitoral hood. Only that spot. The women are known as "the strokees." The explanation is that this high, sub-orgasmic vibration benefits both parties and everyone else in the room. This organization

---

1 No, not that Salma!

has events globally, sometimes with as many as a thousand people taking part. I try not to judge, but have little interest in further exploring this, or touching (gloved or not) a sea of middle-aged, divorced office manager vaginas. Still, I politely listen.

After the talk, the blonde equine woman with the disquieting stare approaches me. She's wearing an ill-fitting black dress with pet hair all over it. She's unkempt with messy hair and bad skin. She's in her late 30s.

EQUINE: I couldn't help but notice that you were trying to get my attention.

If by trying to get your attention, you mean avoiding eye contact, then yes. Trying to be polite…

ME: Um. I thought you were trying to get MY attention, so… anyway. I'm just supporting my friend Salma.

EQUINE LADY: Would you like to sign up for our men's introductory class? It's $375 for three hours and you'll get to stroke someone at the end.

I was uncomfortable and at a loss for words. When people try to aggressively sell me anything, I shut down.

ME: No, thank you.

EQUINE LADY: (Rolling her eyes) Ugh!

She stomped off in a clippity cloppity clumsy canter and I couldn't wait to get the fuck out of this thing.

I didn't know what to say to Salma. My tendency is to joke about anything that makes me uncomfortable.

SALMA: So, what did you think?

ME: It's… interesting, but if you wanted a hand job, all you had to do was ask. Not sure if you know this, but Nathan means "giver" in Hebrew.

SALMA: Funny, but it's not about sex or orgasms. It's about connecting with people and reaching a higher vibration.

Whatever the fuck ever. I don't even like groups of people who are dressed. I'm just not a groups person.

ME: I'm gonna walk up to Canters and get some soup.

"

We made our way into Ivanka's tent. She was on the phone. She was wearing nothing but a pair of silver heels.

Chapter Twenty-Five

The Two Times I Met Ivanka Trump

The first time I met Ivanka Trump was at New York Fashion Week in the late '90s. I was with a friend who was a modeling agent. We were backstage at Marc Jacobs at the Armory. All the biggest supermodels, past and present, were there. Mostly wearing nothing but heels, smoking cigarettes, and sipping from splits of Veuve Clicquot through black straws so as not to smear their lipstick. I was shooting TMAX 3200-speed black-and-white film through a black Contax G2 rangefinder. She motioned for me to come to her.

GIANNA: We have to go see another one of my models for a meeting. She's in another show and has her own private tent.

ME: Who's bigger than these girls? Who gets a private tent here?

GIANNA: Ivanka Trump. She doesn't want to change with photographers around.

ME: Oh, OK. Hey. At the risk of sounding stupid, why do you manage her? Why isn't she repped by Trump Models?

GIANNA: (Rolling her eyes and exhaling a plume of silver cigarette smoke) Please, sweetheart.

This was her pure Italian way of telling me that Trump Models was a joke. A low-grade, junior varsity operation. This was common knowledge, but I was still surprised she wasn't the face of her father's agency. She said much worse and more salacious things about the agency, but since I can't prove any of them, I won't put it here.

We made our way into Ivanka's tent. She was on the phone. She was wearing nothing but a pair of silver heels. She waved and gave us her trademark big, horsey, veneered smile and pointed to her phone, articulating she'd be right with us. Now, I know the rules in this sort of situation. Keep your eyes upstairs. Act natural. She looked great, and in great shape. She was gracious. The meeting was maybe 15 minutes and was mostly about show scheduling for the next few days.

The second time I met Ivanka was after a day of golf with a friend at Bel-Air Country Club. It was an early tee time and I of course managed to dribble some coffee on my white polo. I'll play with a dirty shirt at a municipal dog track, but not here, so I headed into the pro shop to buy a fresh one.

I was headed home when I got a call from a friend we'll call Aaron. Aaron is now a pop megastar. I knew him and the guys in his band for years before they had a record deal. I had seen them play shows where there were more people onstage than in the audience. He was finally hitting his stride, and he had just bought his first Hollywood Hills bachelor pad and I was super stoked for him.

AARON: Where are you?

ME: Coming down Bellagio. You?

AARON: Swing by. Having a few friends over for a BBQ.

ME: En route.

I was sweaty, but still looked good in my best golf clothes. White shirt. Black tailored trousers, white wing tips, and black glove. I headed across town and up Beachwood Canyon in Hollywood Hills East.

As I walked into the house, I saw a guy we'll call Jay, a guitarist. Next to him was Ivanka.

JAY: Hey bro. Do you know Ivanka?

ME: (Shaking her hand) Yes. We've met before.

IVANKA: (Smiling) Yes! Where?

ME: (Also smiling) I almost didn't recognize you with your clothes on!

Now I don't know why these things slip out of my mouth. It's like Tourettes. I've always been this way. I tease. I kid, but I care. The look on his face was not amused. Her brow furrowed. Before it went south, I needed to reel this one back in.

JAY: You've seen her naked?

ME: As the DAY she was born.

IVANKA: (Laughing, thankfully) Where have you seen me naked?

ME: Backstage. Bryant Park with Gianna.

IVANKA: Oh my god. That's my old agent. (To Jay) He's totally seen me naked. (To me) I totally thought you were gay!

ME: I totally thought that you totally thought I was gay.

We all laughed...

She noticed the logo on my new shirt and homed in.

IVANKA: Are you a member at Bel-Air?

ME: No, but I play there once or twice a month.

IVANKA: What's your handicap?

ME: Eleven.

IVANKA: I'm a two.

Now I'm going to assume most of you don't know what this means, but a two handicap means her average score, give or take, is two shots over par. Most club pros aren't twos. Most club champions probably aren't twos. To be a two, you need a lifetime of practice, loads of natural talent, and the time to play and practice several times per week. Year round. Tiger Woods in his prime was a plus four. Only three shots a side better than Ivanka Trump? I don't fucking think so.

ME: (Irritated) You're not a two.

IVANKA: (Laughing sarcastically) Yes. I am.

ME: If you were a two, I'd know it.

IVANKA: You know everyone's handicaps?

ME: Not everyone's, but if you were a two, I would know. Everyone would know.

I knew I was being an asshole and probably a bad houseguest, but golf is one thing you should never EVER lie about. It's the only pro sport where players call penalties on themselves. It's a game of civility and honor. We remove our hats when we shake hands. She had to be called out.

She changed the subject.

IVANKA: Have you ever played my family's course in Palos Verdes?

ME: Yes, I have. A few times.

IVANKA: (Honest to God, she said this) You know, a lot of people say it's better than Pebble Beach.

Oh fuck off. The only thing Trump National and Pebble Beach Golf Links have in common is that they're both touching the Pacific Ocean. Pebble is a legendary U.S. Open venue built in 1919. Trump National is 18 holes on a piece of land big enough for 15. It's in decent shape, but it sucks. Trash architecture. No style, and it has never hosted a single PGA Tour event and never will. It's just a really average, narrow, tacky resort course.

ME: (Shaking my head no) Nobody has *ever* once said that.

She was being a pretty good sport considering I just called her a liar to her face.

IVANKA: (Laughing) You think I'm a big blowhard, don't you? We should play sometime.

ME: (Laughing) The apple doesn't fall too far from the tree. Let's play tomorrow.

IVANKA: Sure. Do you want to play for money?

I'm not a gambler. That stress kind of takes the fun out of the game for me. I didn't have much money to bet or lose at this point in my life, but there was no way I was going to lose to her with nine shots. No. Way. I was playing three to four times per week. My swing was grooved and my short game, surgical. Above all, I saw bullshit in her eyes.

ME: Sure. Your course. You give me nine shots. A thousand a hole?

IVANKA: Give me your number and if I can make it, I'll call you in the morning.

She never called.

"

"First floor, sushi bar. Second floor, streep club. Third floor, casino. Fourth floor, streep club. Fifth floor, streep club."

Chapter Twenty-Six

Kidnapped in Kyiv

A few years back, I got a call from a college friend.

He'd call me every few months from his Upper East Side penthouse and kvetch about how bored he was since getting forced out of Morgan Stanley with a $72 million dollar severance package. Poor bastard.

ALEXEI: Scotty, I want to show you where I grew up.

ME: Kyiv? Yeah. Let's go sometime.

ALEXEI: Fuck sometime. Let's go Thursday.

ME: Dude, I'm an artist. I can't just buy a last-minute plane ticket to Ukraine.

ALEXEI: Shut up. Take down my credit card number and I'll see you there.

I arrived at our hotel, fucked from jet lag in the middle of the night, walked to the front desk and handed the attendant my passport. I can never sleep on planes. Not even in a lie-flat seat, lit up on Scotch and Ambien.

DESK ATTENDANT: Welcome to Kyiv! I am Nikolai.

ME: Hey, Nikolai.

NIKOLAI: *Amerikanski?*

ME: *Da.*

NIKOLAI: What you want do while in Kyiv?

ME: Nikolai. Everything.

NIKOLAI: You want shoot cow with Soviet Bazooka?

ME: (Laughing, loving this guy already) That's your opener?

NIKOLAI: *Shtua?*

ME: Nothing. While it would make a hell of a slow motion YouTube video, I'm going to have to say *nyet* to that one.

NIKOLAI: You want shoot real Kalashnikov AK-47?

Is this guy my soulmate?

ME: Nikolai. I'm American. I have more guns personally than you have in this entire city.

NIKOLAI: Hokay. You want go to nice club tonight? VIP?

ME: Yeah. Sounds good. We'll be down at 9:30.

NIKOLAI: Hokay. I will hyeav car ready. Do NOT take taxi in Kyiv.

I told Alexei when he arrived. We had the presidential suite. It was so big I couldn't throw a football across the living room. *That'll do, pig.*

Waiting for us outside was the most awesomely tacky gangster car the world has ever seen. A pearl-white Maybach with gold rims, grille, and door handles, with heavy bulletproof doors and windows, limo tint, and curtains.

It's a short ride to the club near the Opera House. The requisite shiny suited thugs with the velvet rope were out front.

We walked in and it was an immediate letdown. A styrofoamy-looking fake Etruscan statue spitting water under greenish fluorescent lighting. That and a sushi bar that seated three. It looked more like a Warsaw post office than a cool club.

ME: (Still grumpy from travel) Nikolai. What the fuck is this place?

NIKOLAI: Hokay. First floor, sushi bar. Second floor, streep club. Third floor, casino. Fourth floor, streep club. Fifth floor, streep club. And comrade, everything on table on fifth floor.

ME: Everything on table?

NIKOLAI: *Everything* on table.

It took me a couple of beats to process that one.

ME: Oh. OK.

I looked at Alexei.

ME: Fifth floor?

He nodded in the affirmative. The rest of the place was actually pretty nice. We proceeded to the fifth floor. Our personal goon seated us at the center booth and we ordered a bottle of vodka and a caviar presentation. Y'know…. when in Rome.

They brought out a lineup of girls, maybe 15 of them. I've spent more than half of my adult life looking at beautiful women with a critical eye in a casting room and on set. These were among the most arrestingly beautiful women I've ever seen. There were two basic types there.

The first type was the classic Siberian. Porcelain skin. Ice-blue eyes. White blonde hair and full, bee-stung lips.

The other type was the classic Ukrainian brunette. Think Milla Jovovich on her 18th birthday. Asian features, few curves. Obvious fingerprints of Genghis Khan's 37-year rape-a-thon.

Anyway, we were hammered and slogging through a kilo of (likely counterfeit) Beluga Caviar. Finally, my friend said to me…

ALEXEI: Hey. Would you judge me if ONE time in my life, I wanted to be with a woman other than my wife?

They had been together since they were teenagers.

ME: Brother, I am without judgment. Do whatever you like, but if you're going to cheat, I implore you to make it memorable. In fact, I won't support it otherwise.

ALEXEI: Memorable how?

ME: Three at a time. Five at a time. Live like a czar.

ALEXEI: What could I possibly do with three girls at once?

Without skipping a beat, I started rattling off half a dozen generic porn scenarios. He was incredulous.

ALEXEI: I've never thought of any of those things. I'll do two. You're good at talking to women. Will you set it up?

ME: I don't speak Russian or Ukrainian. You do.

ALEXEI: C'mon. Please?

I looked down at his wallet on the table and asked:

ME: I'll try. May I?

ALEXEI: Take whatever you need.

I opened his black crocodile-skin wallet to discover a very thick stack of 500 Euro notes.

ME: They make 500 Euro notes?

He laughed.

ME: OK. In your opinion, who are the two most beautiful women in this entire place?

Without pause, he pointed.

ALEXEI: Those two.

One green-eyed brunette. Hair just past her shoulders. Good curling-iron work. Curvy and petite. One ice blonde. Tall, slim, small breasted, like a runway model. Ripped abs. Small hips. A Greyhound.

Barely able to walk, I approached them.

ME: Hello, ladies!

GIRLS: Hyeloo!

ME: (Sitting and placing the two 500 Euro notes on the table.) Um, would the two of you be willing to have sex with each other and my friend over there if I gave you each one of these?

Their eyes widened and then they enthusiastically nodded yes. Perhaps not my most compelling pitch, but right tool for the job.

Still fried from jet lag, I decided I'd hang back and keep drinking until I got tired. I sent them back and asked them to send the hotel car back to wait for me. Forty-five minutes later, I was bored and left. Alex had booked a regular room in case one of us needed the big suite to himself. Not wanting to interrupt their party, I went back to the regular room.

Another 30 minutes had gone by and I started getting worried. *Did he get kidnapped? Robbed? Do I knock on the door? Do I text him?*

Just then, my phone rang and it was a FaceTime call from Alexei. I answered immediately.

He was on his back and holding the phone straight up in the air from bed smiling so broadly, he looked Chinese. On either side of him were the girls wearing fluffy white hotel robes and smoking the $25 Cohiba cigars I bought at the Duty Free at London Heathrow.

ME: Dude. Are you OK?

ALEXEI: Scotty!!!

ME: Dude. Are you OK?

ALEXEI: OK? Scotty! This is the single greatest moment of my entire LIFE!

ME: (Laughing before speaking in a sarcastic tone) What about the birth of your first child?

ALEXEI: That was pretty amazing too, but this is SO much better!!!

ME: Glad I could help.

ALEXEI: Come to the room.

ME: Eh. I don't want to rain on your parade.

ALEXEI: I already fucked them twice. Come over!

I returned to the big suite. It looked like a rock band had trashed it. It stunk of spilled liquor and cigar smoke. Pretty much the whole room service menu had been ordered. I saw a half-eaten cheeseburger, a deceased shrimp cocktail, half an omelet, and an empty bottle of Cristal upside down in the melted ice bucket.

They came out of the bedroom and we hung out and partied for a couple of hours. The sun was beginning to rise, and I was getting both sober and hungry.

ME: I'm going downstairs to hit the Sunday brunch. Anyone?

ALEXEI: Should we ask the girls?

ME: Sure. Bring 'em.

They chatted in Russian, got dressed, and we headed for the elevator.

As we entered the restaurant, it looked like any Western high-end hotel brunch. A guy carving a roast beef, a penguin ice sculpture with peeled shrimp and oysters, a sushi guy… the usual.

I looked at the girls. They looked stunned. Frozen. Freaked out.

ME: Hey. Yulia. You OK?

YULIA: (Strong Russka accent) Soooo. How does thees work?

ME: I don't understand. How does what work?

YULIA: We take food and you pay for what we eat?

ME: Yes, we pay and it's all you can eat.

YULIA: It ees impossible.

ME: What's impossible?

YULIA: I can eat as much sushi as I like? Take as many shrimp and oysters as I like? Drink as much champagne as I like?

ME: Babe. Eat a fishing boat.

We sat down, then grabbed plates and headed to the buffet. They were stacking their plates to an embarrassing height.

ME: (Gesturing to put those plates down and start again) You know. You can come back as many times as you like.

JENYA: Oh. Hokay. Sank you.

We were eating, drinking, and having a good time. As we neared the end of the meal, Jenya asked:

JENYA: Sooo, you want historical tour of city? We are architecture students at university.

ME: Oh, yes! I would love that. I love history. Alexei?

They took us all over town. Explained the history of the city. The era when it was called Kievan Rus, the capital of all of Russia. The war. Stalinist architecture, history of the churches. Great tour. Very smart and cool sex workers.

ALEXEI: Scotty. Let's take them shopping at the mall.

ME: Your money.

We went to the mall and Alexei hooked them up. He bought them both iPads. Then bought Yulia a Louis Vuitton dog carrier. (She was blonde, had a Chihuahua, and was a huge Paris Hilton fan. We called her Paris for the rest of the day.) Jenya went for a classic navy Chanel quilted bag. Timeless, solid choices. We part ways.

DAY TWO

We were sightseeing and covering a lot of ground. We hired an actual tour guide to take us around. It was a hot, humid, and cloudless day. We walked and took a lot of taxis. I told Alexei what Nikolai said about never taking taxis. He scoffed:

ALEXEI: *You* don't take taxis, Yankee. *I do.*

A friend of mine who was an advertising Chief Executive saw on my Facebook that I was in Kyiv and offered to tee up a meeting at his local outpost. It was nice of him, but it turned out to be kind of a bust. The vast majority of this office's work was repurposing artwork from the West and slapping on Ukrainian translations of slogans. They offered me a job for an airline and a vodka brand, but it would have been a month out and break even at best, kind of like shooting celebrities.

I was walking back to the hotel. Uphill. Hot day.

Kyiv, from what I could glean, was all about altitude. All the good shit was on their Mulholland Drive. As you descended down the hill, it looked less desirable. At the bottom of the hill was the Dnieper River, and that area looked like shit. Not like Hollywood Boulevard shit, but a different, more desolate kind of shit. Like where one would find dead bodies and Nazi artifacts from the war.

The ad agency was a bit downhill from the hotel, but not so much so. Either way, I was sweating, hungover, and exhausted. I decided to take a taxi. It was less than a ten-minute drive.

I got in the car and told him the hotel. He turned around, sized me up, and the first words out of his mouth were:

CAB DRIVER: Real Rolex?

I knew I shouldn't have worn this big gold hunk of criminal catnip on my wrist...

ME: Oh. This? No! Fake. Canal Street. New York City.

This guy was not buying it. At all. Like he even knew what the fuck Canal Street is.

He continued driving. After a few minutes I noticed we were going down the hill. *Maybe he's taking a shortcut?*

ME: Hey. Comrade, go back up.

CAB DRIVER: (Turning and pointing at me) SIT!

ME: Stop the fucking car!

He started driving faster down the hill. Coasting through stop signs and lights.

Finally, we were on the banks of the Dnieper. Shit hole. Graffiti. Trash. The perfect place to dump my body.

Then he got on the freeway headed out of town. We were in a Lada. A piece of shit Soviet tin can of a car that was based on a Fiat 124, but wasn't half the car the Fiat was (and that was a huge Italian pile of shit).

We were going faster and faster and the car felt like it was going to fall apart at speed. Now I was panicking. *Will he just take my watch and my phone and ditch me? Will it be ransom? Will he sell me to the mob? Kill me?* I'm not a worrier, but I was fucking worried.

I needed a plan and I needed it fast. I was looking around to try and make eye contact with anyone. Then, out the windshield, I noticed a police car ahead and immediately thought, *There's no way this guy is going to pass a police car while speeding.* But alas, he did.

The moment we passed the cop car, I rolled down my window. Threw the two floor mats out the window, followed by the stack of magazines and books on the rear window ledge. Glad this guy was a slob. The cop immediately pulled us over. Thank God!

I was shaking and freaking out.

ME: Officer. This motherfucker tried to kidnap me!

The cop listened, but didn't seem to care. He was examining the guy's driver's license. The guy looked impatient. Cab driver wouldn't even look at me.

ME: Excuse me. Officer?

He walked away. Ignored again.

Finally, the driver's patience had run out and, bizarrely, he snatched his license back from the cop's hand and started walking back to his car. The cop body slammed him and cuffed him. Everything was in slow motion. The driver was sitting on the curb cuffed. Cop still talking on his radio.

I was still boiling over with adrenaline.

ME: Officer. This man tried to kidnap me!

COP: *Amerikanski?*

ME: *Da.*

COP: Why you take taxi in Kyiv?

ME: I know. My hotel told me not to, but…

COP: You are stupid eediot.

ME: (Taking it) I know. Can you please give me a ride back to the hotel?

COP: *Nyet.* You are imbecile. You walk back. Learn lesson.

Is this guy for real?

ME: Can you please call my hotel and tell them where I am so they can pick me up?

COP: *Nyet.* You walk back. You are stupid man.

The guy got arrested and they left me on the side of the highway. I didn't have a local SIM card so I started taking the heel-and-toe express back down the highway and up the mountain. It was four miles easy up a steep hill. Over 80 degrees, and I was hungover and dehydrated.

After 45 minutes, I needed water and rest. I saw a place with a mural of Che Guevara on the side. It was a cigar lounge. I bought a cigar in the hope of getting some help.

ME: (To waitress) Wi-Fi? (Pronounced "weefee" here.)

Her English was minimal. I handed her my phone. She logged me onto the Wi-Fi. I wrote a note in Google translate and explained what happened. She called the hotel for me from the bar phone. It was Nikolai. I explained briefly what happened.

NIKOLAI: Mr. Scott. I *tell* you not take taxi in Kyiv. You are stupid idiot!

If ONE more person calls me that today…

ME: I know! Can you please come pick me up?

NIKOLAI: Your friend very worried. I connect.

ME: Wait! No!

ALEXEI: Scotty, where the fuck have you been?

ME: I took a taxi and got briefly kidnapped. No big deal.

ALEXEI: Idiot. I told you not to…

ME: Dude. *Don't.* I'll see you soon.

66

"During dinner, he pulled out a bullet that literally had 'NATHAN' written on it in Sharpie."

Chapter Twenty-Seven

The Military Contractor's Wife

Summer, 2010

A lawyer friend asked me to be her plus-one at her New England prep school's 20-year reunion. Sometimes it feels like I'm everyone's plus-one.

It was at a fellow alum and his wife's home in Brentwood Park. There was a black Ferrari Scuderia and a black Tesla S in the driveway. Chic.

I became social media friends with both of them and took the husband to the gun club once. There, I asked him what he did for work. He said he provided satellite internet infrastructure for the military in war-torn countries. Sure. Why not? No reason not to believe him.

As it turns out, he was a con man and had been living off of investors he'd fleeced with this same pitch.

A year later, on my way into a meeting, I ran into his wife in the lobby of The Four Seasons. She mentioned that she and her husband were now divorced. She gave me her number, suggesting we grab lunch sometime. We had lunch, then later that week, dinner at my place, where I cooked a Rocky Mountain elk tenderloin that a friend had hunted. She stayed over and filled me in on how it all went down.

It all went tits up while she was checking out at Trader Joe's, and her credit card was declined. Within a few minutes, the rest of her cards were declined. Later that night she and her husband were having dinner at Peppone, a red sauce joint in Brentwood. She was nervous about bringing it up in conversation, then finally did at the end of the meal.

KAYLEIGH: So, all my credit cards were declined today at the grocery store.

CHASE: Yeah. Don't use those. They're never going to work again.

He explained that the whole business was fake. Made up. They were broke and had nothing left. They had two kids each from previous marriages.

KAYLEIGH: What are we going to do?

CHASE: We? I'm moving back in with my mother. It's you I'm worried about.

Post-coital conversation:

KAYLEIGH: Scott, do you ever wonder what people think about you for having never been married?

ME: Maybe I haven't met her yet. Do you ever wonder what people think about your being divorced three times?

She continued with this shitty negative attitude, so I politely told her I didn't think we were a fit.

Two months later, my friend Marissa had just gotten back from a first date with the ex-husband.

MARISSA: Do you know this guy named Chase?

ME: Yeah, I know him. Why?

MARISSA: Did you know he is planning to kill you?

ME: Hilarious. Get in line.

MARISSA: He said you fucked his ex-wife.

ME: Accurate. Once. She's a bad person.

MARISSA: He's a freak. You should be careful. During dinner, he pulled out a bullet that literally had "NATHAN" written on it in Sharpie.

ME: How dramatic. I'm unconcerned. People who are actually going to kill people don't go around telling people they're going to kill them. When I took him to the gun club, he not only borrowed my guns because he didn't own any, but also couldn't hit the side of a barn.

Later that night:

MARISSA: I talked him down. He's not going to kill you.

ME: Don't interfere.

MARISSA: What?

ME: Maybe it's my fate.

MARISSA: Don't be an idiot, Scott.

"

*If porn had a Mount Rushmore,
Jenna Jameson would
certainly be on it.*

Chapter Twenty-Eight

Priests and Porn Stars

In the year 2000, I owned a web design agency. That year we only had two clients: a large television Christian ministry and Jenna Jameson's Clubjenna.com, a porn site that was the most expensive acquisition in the history of adult and may still be.

Before we took on Clubjenna.com, We were maxed out and couldn't take any more business.

The Christian client was a mega church that was the scale a professional sports arena. Needless to say, this long-haired Jewish biker felt more than a bit out of place.

In the late '90s, we'd had a great run producing websites for major motion pictures, television, properties, and fashion brands. It was the golden age of web development. Six-figure paydays and four- to six-week turnarounds. I was working half days, and we were smashing it.

By 2000, all of our work was focused on this massive television ministry.

One day, I got a call from a guy who was married to Jenna Jameson saying he liked our work and wanted to meet.

ME: I'm sorry, but I can't do your website.

HUSBAND: Why? Are you anti porn or super Christian?

ME: No. I like porn as much as the next guy or girl. It's that I have women who work for me and I don't want to force them to look at porn all day.

HUSBAND: We have a lot of money.

ME: So does Disney.

HUSBAND: We're flying into LA next week. Just meet with me and Jenna and reserve judgment.

I'm not going to lie. Jenna is an icon and I wanted to take the meeting just for the story. So did my business partner. So did everyone at the ad agency we were working out of. If porn had a Mount Rushmore, Jenna Jameson would certainly be on it.

JENNA: I want you to do my site.

ME: Jenna, I can't do a porn site. I don't have any secrets, and my other clients would hate it. So would most of the women who work for us.

JENNA: It's going to be more of a lifestyle site. Kind of like *Martha Stewart Living*.

ME: No porn?

JENNA: Yes. Porn, but it won't *look* like a porn site. Look, I'll pay you a lot of money.

ME: My other clients pay me a lot of money and they're Fortune 100 companies. I can't do it, Jen.

JENNA: Just start another entity under a different name that just does my site.

ME: Hmm.

JENNA: Listen. I'll give you $125,000 dollars and will write you a check for half of it now.

ME: (Extending my hand and smiling) Welcome to the family, Jenna.

"

Almost everyone owns the same car: a white Chevy Suburban. After a few visits, I finally asked someone why.

Chapter Twenty-Nine

"Russel Crowe" and the Zoomers in Mexico

Winter, 2014

A group of us flew down to a friend's home in Costa Careyes, Mexico. "Careyes," as it's known, is a beautiful little town of colorful and architectural vacation homes owned by Hollywood stars, wealthy Americans, European expats, and a few fun-loving international criminals. I had visited a handful of times over the past few years and stayed at a couple different homes.

It's a real community. Everyone knows everyone. So much so that I wouldn't want to live there for that reason. There are no hotels or resorts that I know of. Every night there's a dinner party at a different house and it's the same 30 or so people at each of them.

One interesting tidbit about Careyes is that almost everyone owns the same car: a white Chevy Suburban. After a few visits, I finally asked someone why.

As it turns out, the narco traffickers all drive black Chevy Suburbans. The white ones signify "civilian." The agreement is that drug traffickers can keep their trade routes, but if anyone in a white Suburban gets messed with, the deal is off and all hell breaks loose.

This visit was over the Christmas/New Year holiday. A couple of attractive Gen Z influencer, sugar types had been invited by someone on this trip. Not to "perform" but more as pool and party decor, and to tart the place up a bit. We met on the plane ride out. They were perfectly nice, despite Snapchatting their every move and constantly talking to their phone screens like psych patients.

On the night of New Year's Eve, there was a party with 400 or so guests. The finest tequila, molly, and uncut cocaine flowed. I stuck with the booze and was chatting with an older French couple when the girls came over to me in their string bikinis.

GIRLS: Oh my God, Scott. Did you see? Russell Crowe is here.

Behind them in the crowd, maybe 30 feet away, I saw Gerard Butler. I didn't know him well, but had met him a handful of times in LA via mutual friends and had already said a quick hello.

ME: Where?

They gestured to Gerry talking to a few people. I was tipsy and feeling naughty.

ME: Oh, good. He made it. Yes. I invited him.

GIRLS: Will you introduce us?

ME: Of course, but if there's one thing I know about Russell Crowe, it's that he loves when people compliment his work. Here's what you do. Walk up to him and tell him you loved him in *A Beautiful Mind* and *Master and Commander*.

GIRLS: Really? Are you sure he won't just think we're creepy fans?

ME: Definitely not. You're hot girls, he's a down to earth Australian and he will LOVE it.

They walked over. Gerry was smiling and turning on the charm. That smile quickly faded to a "what the fuck?" head shake.

Pleased with myself, I walked away. Sorry, G.B.

"

*Face down and in fear of
getting shot… What could've
been worse than that?*

Chapter Thirty

The Thong Bank Robbery

2001, 2 p.m.

An M.A.W. (model actress whatever) friend called, frantic and hyperventilating.

ME: What's wrong? What happened?

CARLY: I was just in a bank robbery at the Bank of America on Fairfax!

ME: Like an armed robbery? With guns and masks?

CARLY: Yes!

ME: Jesus. That must have been harrowing. How long was the ordeal?

CARLY: I'm not sure, but it seemed like forever.

ME: I'm sure. I can't imagine being face down and in fear of getting shot.

CARLY: That wasn't even close to the worst part.

ME: What could've been worse than that?

CARLY: I was wearing a tiny plaid miniskirt and a thong and it got hiked all the way up over my ass when we were all ordered to the ground. I really wanted to pull it down to cover myself, but was afraid they would kill me. All I could think about was all of the cops and FBI laughing at my bare white ass in a hot pink thong in the surveillance video and laughing at me. That's still all I'm thinking about.

And, scene…

> *Beginner's luck, I guess.*
> *I submitted this as an app store*
> *review, but it was rejected.*

Chapter Thirty-One

Tinder App Review

2012

My first Tinder date was with a fine art painter by the name of Amy. Thirty-one, athletic, fun, and talented. RISD grad. *New York Times* critic's pick and a ginger.

We had a really fun slumber party on the first date. I liked this app so far.

My second Tinder date was a first assistant director named Sabrina. A cute, curvy, freckled brunette. She worked on some of my favorite films and was interesting to talk filmmaking with. We went out twice in three days and had sex on the second date.

The day after my second date with Sabrina, I got a midday text from Amy.

AMY: Have you ever had a threesome before?

ME: Yes.

ONE minute later, I got the exact same text from Sabrina.

AMY: How many times?

ME: I'm not sure. More than 50, less than 100? I had an ex who was into them and was constantly wrangling people.

They both asked if I knew anyone who might be down to play. Until that moment, I didn't. With nothing whatsoever to lose, I made screenshots of both of their profiles and sent them to each other. They were both interested. *This can't be that easy.*

Amy thought it would be funny for the three of us to meet at a strip club, but deliberately not a nice one.

We all Ubered separately to a dive strip club in North Hollywood. We ordered a plastic pitcher of draft beer and got to know each other between trips to the smoking patio. We were having a great time. Tipping dancers and drinking beer. *This could actually work.*

Spontaneously, the three of us started kissing at the table. Our table was just in front of the stage. Our faces were in a triangular configuration. Suddenly, I felt what I thought was water or something being poured over the top of my hat and I flinched backward.

There were two drunk guys "making it rain" dollar bills over the top of us. The three of us started laughing. The stripper on the stage was scowling and the cocktail waitresses were visibly pissed. I ordered an Uber Suburban. Now was not the time to be cheap.

ME: We should leave.

The girls were in agreement. We gathered all of the dollars around us, hummed them onto the stage, and booked it out of there.

We spent the next couple of days at my place. Beginner's luck, I guess.

I submitted this as an app store review, but it was rejected.

66

Nicolas Cage: "This is a tool I've always used to deal with stressful situations and it works every time without exception."

Chapter Thirty-Two

My Therapist, Nicolas Cage

Winter, 1996, Chicago

It was that time of the year. Twenty degrees below zero wind chill factor. Black skies at 11 a.m. Walking from my parking garage to my office at 232 E. Ohio street. Walking on diesel soot–stained black ice in whipping wind, hearing screams of "fuck this shit," "motherfucker!" and so on.

Every year I wondered why I stayed in this city. Why my family stayed so long. Why my friends stayed. Were it not for the weather, I'd argue that Chicago may be America's best city. Maybe I'm just nostalgic. Your odds of getting shot were lower in those days too. Many things kept me there. Friends, culture, and family. Now I'd had enough.

I had recently returned from vacation with a childhood friend. It was one of those cheapie Cancun all-inclusive packages that college students on limited budgets take. He planned it and it was just what I needed— a week of sunshine, beer, and tequila.

Our return flight had been delayed due to weather till late that night. The good news was that we got a full extra day in Mexico. The bad news, we had to move out of our rooms and store our luggage with everyone else's in a hospitality suite.

Genius that I was, I left my passport in my bag with my original birth certificate inside. They were stolen together. This was pre 9/11 and one only needed a driver's license to return to the States.

Back in my office on that dark, dreary, frozen Monday, I contemplated a massive life change. I needed to move. It was time. First call of the day was to the Department of Vital Statistics to order a replacement birth certificate. They informed me that since I was adopted (and a closed adoption at that) it was a more complex process than normal. I first had to apply for this document called a "Gold Certificate," which would then enable them to release a newly censored birth certificate.

I finished this process over the next month. I finally got the birth certificate back. It was more or less the same, save for one snippet of information at the bottom of the birth certificate. It had a lawyer's name and a law firm. It was around 6 p.m. and I was in my office. I decided to call the number. A man answered.

MAN: Hello?

ME: I'm sorry. I must have the wrong number. I was trying to reach a law firm.

MAN: This is a law firm. My secretary went home for the day and I picked up. What can I help you with?

ME: I was adopted through this firm in the '60s and wanted to get some information.

MAN: Are you the judge's nephew?

ME: Yes. How did you know that?

MAN: I went to law school with him at John Marshall. We were class-mates. His sister needed a lawyer to do her adoption. I referred it to my father and yours is the only adoption we've ever done.

ME: Wow. Do you have any information about it? I want to find my biological family.

MAN: All I can tell you is that you were adopted via a closed adoption through the Jewish Children's Bureau of Chicago. Try them.

ME: Thanks so much.

I called the agency the following day and chatted with a woman whose sole job was reuniting adopted kids and parents. She explained to me how it all works and not to get my hopes up. She said the odds were low that she could help.

The only way these records could be opened would be if there was permission in my file via a letter from one or both of my birth parents.

She explained that the storage records facility isn't unlike the final shot in *Raiders of the Lost Ark* and it may take her weeks to find paperwork and microfiche in a box. I thanked her and I waited.

Four or five weeks later, she called me back with an update. There were letters written to me by my birth mother. Five of them. All birthday cards beginning at age 13 and as recently as two years prior to this present time. They were all more or less the same message. "Happy Birthday. Should you ever come looking for me, here's the contact info of where I am now."

The lady from the adoption agency said that, given that it had been two years, the trail may have gone cold again. She said she would try to track my mother down at her last known contact info. Three days later, she was found. Neither one of us wanted to give the other their phone number and neither one of us was willing to budge. We finally settled on a plan. My birth mother would go to the agency that Thursday and I would call in at 4:30 p.m.

The conversation was awkward. She was emotional and I got the sense she was not entirely together. I could feel that she had a hard life and struggled with mental illness. We chatted by phone a half dozen or so times over the next couple of weeks. During that time, I had moved to Los Angeles. I wasn't yet ready to meet face to face.

Two months later, I returned to tie up some loose ends. Get my old Harley Davidson out of storage and onto a truck to California and a few other things. I decided it was time to meet her.

Knowing this was my deep and personal journey and not wanting to risk hurting my parents, I decided to keep this all to myself for the time being. The weather was unchanged, a brutal, black, frozen hellscape. I decided to dress like a grownup for my meeting with her. I wore a navy Gianni Versace suit with a colorful Hermès scarf tie (it was the '90s), a black, full-length cashmere topcoat, and a long Raf Simons scarf.

I knew Chicago like the back of my hand, but had no idea where this area was. I asked my father.

ME: Dad, where is the intersection of X and Y?

DAD: I'll tell you where it is. It's where you're not going in your mother's new car. They'll kill you and steal the car. What's there anyway? A club?

ME: Yes. A new club.

DAD: Forget it.

ME: I'll tell the guys we're going someplace else.

I had planned to maybe tell them eventually, but not then. I did, however, tell my thrice-married, exceedingly Botoxed, Judas of a sister who waited all of five minutes to betray me. Nothing new. Just thought I'd give an irredeemable person another shot at redemption.

Off I went to the Northwest side hood in a blizzard to meet my birthing vessel.

At the time, I was an IT guy. I designed networks, produced websites, and did concierge support for demanding clients. My main client was Nicolas Cage at the pinnacle of his career. He'd recently won his Oscar and Golden Globe for best actor and was just starting his rise to summer tentpole action star. He was a great client and a funny and generous guy.

Between his office and a pile of houses, there were a lot of billable hours to be had. Designing and building networks in five residences, as well as lessons for him, his wife Patricia Arquette, his baby mama Christina, his kid Weston, his step-kid, Enzo and his office staff. He was also not the guy you ever just "called back." Day or night, when he called, you picked up.

Nicolas called just as I was feeling very, very nervous about this first-time meeting with this strange woman who gave birth to me. I was never impatient or short with him. Until this moment.

ME: Hey, Nic. *Really* bad time. Anything super urgent?

SILENCE on the other end.

Nic is a lovely guy, but he's still a movie star with a sizable staff and I'm pretty sure he hadn't been told no in a very long time. I caught myself and tried to soften it.

ME: Sorry, what do you need? I'm going through something heavy right now.

NC: What's happening?

ME: I'm in Chicago driving to meet the woman who gave birth to me for the first time and I'm kind of freaking out.

NC: I can help you.

ME: (Squinting and sighing) How?

NC: First of all, do you have any Valium?

ME: Yeah. Way ahead of you. Already on five milligrams.

NC: Perfect. OK. Here's what I want you to do. Are you listening?

ME: I am.

NC: Take yourself out of the first person.

ME: How?

NC: This is a tool I've always used to deal with stressful situations and it works every time without exception.

I pulled the car over.

ME: Go on.

NC: I want you to picture yourself alone in a dark movie theater.

ME: OK.

NC: Get specific. You're sitting in a red velvet theater seat. You're watching a black comedy. It's unfolding before your eyes. It's fascinating and funny. Take it all in, but take yourself out of it.

All of my stress instantly melted away and it wasn't the Valium. Nic Cage, you're a different breed of cat, but you're a fucking genius.

ME: OK. I'm going in.

NC: Good luck.

It was snowing hard. Those big, heavy and wet midwestern snowflakes. Nothing like that light, fluffy and expensive Vail shit. There was a group of vagrants standing around a burning 55-gallon drum. I found a parking space and prayed this brand-new, gleaming black BMW would be covered with snow quickly enough to lessen its chances of being stolen.

I entered the poorly maintained old brick mid-rise building. Trying to breathe and take it in as Cage advised. A legless man in a wheelchair wearing a military jacket whizzed by, his eyes locking with mine in a long pan. The olfactory overtone—the smell of institutional gravy, pine cleaner, and cheap cafeteria food—filled my nostrils. The undertone was the stench of old people.

I noticed the thick layers of dingy paint that may have once been white, but now was a greenish yellow bathed in F40T12/CW light. That is the code for a four-foot, cool white fluorescent tube. How do I know this? My dad made a decent living selling these and their eight-foot counterpart, the F96T12 CW. They made that vomitous green light you never see anymore except in movies about the '70s and '80s.

Moving on, My field of vision was assaulted by all manner of human frailty. I moved toward the front desk and made eye contact with a pie-eyed, strange, grinning woman in her early 60s.

RECEPTIONIST: Praise Jesus! How may I help you?

What the fuck, over? What is this place? (I never exactly found out other than that it was some kind of subsidized housing.)

ME: (At a rare loss for words) Hi, um, I'm here to meet… um.

RECEPTIONIST: You're Dora's son, aren't you?

ME: (Confused) Uh, yes.

RECEPTIONIST: We've all been hearing about you for weeks.

Now my stomach was cramping with anxiety. Listen to Cage. Don't run. Keep going.

I made my way to the elevator area that was packed with a post-dinner crowd. After 10 minutes, I realized that only one of the four elevator banks was working. Every time one opened, the residents pushed and shoved and packed together like sardines. I kept politely waving them through. "Go ahead. I'll get the next one." I was beginning to sweat in my wool suit and topcoat and the dry radiator heat began to suck the juice from my mouth, nose, and eyes.

After 20 minutes, I decided enough was enough. I joined the Hunger Games and shoved my body into the car and took it to the 15th floor. Just like in a movie, she was the last unit at the end of a long, poorly lit hallway. The carpeting was a deep red and black pattern, like an Old West whorehouse/casino. I paused, then rapped my knuckles twice on her door. I heard nervousness in her voice on the other side.

DORA: Oh… hel.… hello?

ME: Hi, It's Scott.

She opened the door to reveal what appeared to be a very tidy dorm room. There was a plywood sleeping loft over a mint green thrift-store loveseat in good shape. Across the room I saw an old mid-century dresser also in good shape with maybe two-dozen prescription pill bottles arranged neatly on top. Nervously, she asked:

DORA: (proudly) Sooo, what do you think of my place?

ME: It's nice.

DORA: You know… It's one of the only units here that has its own bathroom. Can I get you anything? A cigarette? A Percodan?

ME: (Giggling) Did you just offer me a Percodan?

DORA: (With a shrug) Yes.

ME: (I laughed again and pointed) You're my mom, alright!

I loved painkillers in those days.

This was the first time I had ever met any flesh and blood relative, so I was fastidiously studying her every feature. Over the phone, she sounded like my twin, five-foot-eleven, long curly red hair, pale skin, slim with green eyes. In person, I saw no similarity other than that we had the same ugly, ruddy freckled hands. None.

I won't bore you with all of the details, but I asked her if it was OK to interview her, and explained that my memory isn't great and asked if she'd mind my taking notes. She consented. I pulled a yellow legal pad and for an hour or so peppered her with questions about how I came to be.

It was difficult to keep her focused. She was cycling manic and I was learning more about her, and perhaps to a greater extent, my own genetic makeup.

The gist is, she was a teenager and got pregnant by a guy who was already married with a kid on the way. (I met that kid 20 years later in LA.)

I told her that I had made a dinner reservation at The Pump Room. I was making a decent living at the time and thought it would be a nice gesture. The Pump Room was perhaps Chicago's most famous old-school "fancy" restaurant. It was namechecked in Sinatra's "My Kind of Town." It opened in 1938 and closed in 2017. It was rumored that Oprah had her own booth there with an actual *telephone* in it.

ME: We should get going. The weather is bad and we have an 8:30 reservation.

DORA: No, I couldn't possibly go there.

ME: (Sarcastically) You don't like The Pump Room?

DORA: No, I can't go to any restaurant. They will all just remind me of your father.

ME: Wait. So you haven't been to a restaurant since 1965?

DORA: Oh God, no. They would all remind me of him.

Fuck, this is sad. But fuck, I'm also hungry.

ME: C'mon, we'll have a great time. Let's stop thinking and just hop in the car.

Finally, she said she'd only eat at one place. The place where she'd had her last date with my sperm donor. I'd never heard of this place. It's a deli that in these conditions would be an hour minimum in some far-flung western suburb. I called 411 and prayed it didn't exist anymore so we could eat at the fancy place. Sadly, it was still there.

We got in my other mom's new car and—without asking, with the windows closed—she lit a cigarette. It was so cold and wet out that even cracking a window would be an impossibility. I was trying not to flip my shit, but she was refusing to put it out and ashes were swirling all over the car.

During the drive, out of nowhere, she asked:

DORA: Are you feeling any kind of… deep, psychic, familial connection?

ME: Not really, no.

DORA: Me either.

It was quiet for a while with the only sound being the car heater on max, and the wiper blades sweeping the snow from the windshield.

We finally arrived at the empty deli with the same shitty cool whites that lit her building. The room was replete with '70s fake wood paneling and faded photographs of middle of the road Chicago celebrities, like Jim Belushi and Joe Mantegna on the wall. I was trying to have a meaningful conversation with her and all she could talk about was the menu. I'm not patient on my best day, but was doing my damnedest and I was wondering if I had gotten what I needed from this meeting already.

DORA: Maybe the brisket? Or chicken in the pot? Or a corned beef sandwich? Or the kasha varnishkas, or the latkes? What do you think?

I was kind of already over it.

ME: (Irritated but patient) Get whatever you like. My treat.

The waitress made her way over and it was the same thing all over again. Maybe it's my character flaw, but I hate people who keep servers at the table and batter them with questions, flirt, or start conversations. Shut up, order, and let them get back to work.

DORA: (To waitress) So, between these six things, which is the best?

WAITRESS: (On cue) Well, it depends on what you're in the mood for...

Another five straight minutes of deliberative babbling. I had a minor fit.

ME: (Raising a hand) You know what? Bring us all six of those dishes. She'll take home the leftovers. Thank you.

I got through the rest of it, learned what I needed to, and dropped her off. We spoke a couple more times by phone and that was that. She incubated me and for that I'm grateful, but she's not someone I felt the need to have protracted relationship with.

> 66
>
> *Hey, aren't you John Malkovich's agent? Have you heard of this script called "Being John Malkovich"?*

Chapter Thirty-Three

Being John Malkovich

During my time as a concierge IT guy, I received a referral to a female theatrical agent at a big three agency. We'll call her Shari. When I walked in the door of her house she tried to kiss me. Weird.

ME: Hey, whoa. I'm just the IT guy.

SHARI: What? Do I disgust you? Do I make you sick?

When things go that sideways, it's best to keep going and not add to the weirdness. I stayed calm, warm, and friendly and kept walking into her house.

ME: C'mon. We're not doing that. Show me your computer problem.

I managed to calm her down and fix her issue quickly. She had a beautiful Spanish in Nichols Canyon and a couple of jumpy rescue dogs reflective of their owner's personality. We became friends-ish. She would summon me. We'd drink single malt, BS, and watch *E! News*. Sometimes we'd go shopping.

Everyone knew her and kissed her ass. She would be rude and talk down to almost all of them. She was powerful, lonely, and very very damaged. She would abuse her assistants in person and on the phone.

One afternoon she called:

SHARI: What're you doing later?

ME: Nothing.

SHARI: Johnny Depp just brought over a box of Bolivar Belicosos Finos. Do you know what they are?

ME: Yes. I'm not a philistine. Fifty-two-ring-gauge Havana torpedo. A good one.

SHARI: Come over at 7:30.

Earlier that day, I had to fix some networking issues at a film production company. I was chatting with the development exec and asked him for something to read. I'm paraphrasing the conversation.

D-GUY: What do you want to read?

ME: Something funny.

D-GUY: Does it matter if it's something that will never get made? I have one of those I think you'd like.

ME: I don't care. I just want to be entertained. What is it?

D-GUY: It's hard to explain, but I think you'll like it. It was passed on by everyone and it's been dead for ages. I love this writer. His name is Charlie Kaufman. Super weird.

I went home and read the script in just over an hour and loved it.

I arrived at Shari's at 7:30. We lit the cigars on the back patio. Their construction and draw were flawless with a lovely oily wrapper. We smoked them and drank Highland Park 12 for a couple of hours when the idea struck me.

ME: Hey, aren't you John Malkovich's agent?

SHARI: Yes. Why?

ME: Have you heard of this script called "Being John Malkovich"?

SHARI: (barking) Yeah. I passed on it ages ago. Stupid idea.

ME: Oh, OK.

We continued to watch TV. Twenty minutes passed.

SHARI: Why did you ask me about that script?

ME: I got it from a client and read it today.

SHARI: (Dismissively) You fix computers. Why the fuck are you reading dead screenplays?

ME: I wanted something to read and didn't feel like going to a bookstore. Did you ever read it?

SHARI: Fuck, no. Who reads screenplays?

ME: So, John never heard about it.

SHARI: No. John lives a quiet life in Marseilles.

ME: OK.

SHARI: Was it any good?

ME: It's amazing.

SHARI: Should I send it to John?

ME: Yes.

SHARI: If he hates this and fires me, I will destroy you.

This is the way she talks. You get numb to the aggression.

ME: Yeah yeah. Blah blah blah. (Gesturing with my hand) If you don't send it to him, you're the worst agent ever.

It was 11 p.m. Shari called one of her two assistants, who sounded asleep.

SHARI: Hey. I need you to go to the office right now. Find the latest draft of "Being John Malkovich," drive to the airport, and pouch it to John in France.

ASSISTANT: I thought we passed on that years ago. Can this wait until morning?

SHARI: Do what I fucking say or I'll find someone who will.

Two days later I get an echoey speaker phone call from Shari.

SHARI: You're not going to fucking believe this. John read the script. He immediately connected with it and it's going to be made.

ME: Glad I could help.

SHARI: You have no idea how difficult it is to get him to commit to anything.

At no point was there any thank you or acknowledgment.

ME: Cool. So, can you get me an associate producing credit or something on it?

Shari just hung up the phone. I knew I was screwed, so I decided to be funny and call her back.

SHARI: WHAT?

ME: How about a muffin basket?

She hung up again. Around the time of the film's release, I read an interview with that bearded gasbag Francis Coppola taking credit for it.

Showbiz.

Being John Malkovich went on to receive the 2000 "Best Screenplay" nominations in both the Academy Awards and Golden Globes, as well as win a BAFTA award and a few others.

You're welcome, Charlie Kaufman.

"

A man with a knife stepped out sideways from a building gap: "Your watch and your wallet, señor."

Chapter Thirty-Four

So... One Time... I Committed This Felony...

1994

I was a new arrival in Angel City. No job. No money. Couch surfing. Getting work of any kind was proving significantly tougher than I thought.

Trying to meet some people, I went into an AOL chat room one night and started talking to this woman. She told me she was a comic performing at the Improv on Melrose Avenue that night. There were no jpgs back then. No digital cameras. It was a black-and-white digital classified ad. Friends, fine. Date, fine. Nothing, fine. Don't care. Just get me out of the house.

I showed up having no idea what she'd look like. Without going into too much detail, it wasn't really an aesthetic or personality fit. Oh, and she wasn't really a comic either. She was "The Fluffer," or announcer there to warm up the crowd. She was neither attractive, nor in any way talented. Nevertheless, I saw magic in a just-starting-out Sarah Silverman.

I was walking east on Melrose Avenue. Perhaps a block and a half away. While Melrose appears at first glance to be a series of interconnected, mud-and-chicken-wire, no-civic-pride, sub-Tijuana architecture, some of the buildings have narrow spaces between them.

A man with a knife stepped out sideways from a building gap:

ROBBER: Your watch and your wallet, *señor.*

This nervous-looking, late-20s, diminutive Mexican man with a peach fuzz mustache, didn't seem like a scary felon. Just a dumb ass with a bad idea. Nevertheless, I was on edge.

Having been carjacked at gunpoint in Chicago less than a year earlier, I was quite traumatized. A jumpy crackhead asshole who shoves the barrel of a gun in your mouth while wearing Groucho glasses tends to do that to you. It took a decade before I'd get into someone's convertible or allow windows open in a car.

I wasn't nervous this time. I was ready.

ME: Whoa! OK. I'm just reaching for my wallet, OK?

The robber nodded OK.

I reached for the inside pocket of my leather jacket and pulled out my pocket pistol. A Sig Sauer P230 packed full of Federal Hydra-Shok jacketed hollow points and trained it on the center of his forehead.

ME: Your watch and *your* wallet.

The guy dropped his Chinese liquor store knife, which clattered onto the sidewalk. He took a step back and raised his hands with his elbows at his side.

ROBBER: *Ma señor,* I only have a few coins.

ME: I'll take 'em.

He handed me a quarter, two dimes, and two pennies. Turned and began to walk away.

ME: Where do you think you're going?

ROBBER: I give you everything.

ME: No, you didn't. Give me your wallet and your keys.

ROBBER: (Showing me his open wallet) See? No money.

ME: Give it to me. Part of your punishment is going to the DMV and getting a new license. And your keys.

He handed me his wallet.

ROBBER: You can't take my keys, man, I've got a family. I gotta get home.

ME: Or I can blow a hole in your face. Up to you. Walk home. You're a terrible parent.

He dropped the keys into my open hand, then turned to walk away again.

ME: What are you doing?

ROBBER: Man. What do you want? I give you everything.

ME: No, you didn't. Give me your coat.

ROBBER: You're gonna take my coat?

ME: I'm letting you keep your shoes. That's about it. Any problem with that?

Silence as he hands me his coat.

ME: Now apologize.

ROBBER: Huh.

ME: Tell me you're sorry and you're never going to do this to anyone again.

ROBBER: *I'm sorry.*

He walked away. I threw his keys down the sewer, his coat and his wallet into a dumpster, and felt at the time like I'd somehow done some good.

66

For those of you who don't know, Nathan in Hebrew means "giver" and give I did.

Chapter Thirty-Five

Jobs

Winter, 2013

I was dating a hedge fund manager. It seemed too good to be true She ticked all of my boxes, or so it seemed. She was a smart, funny, beautiful Ivy Leaguer who had an aircraft that could fly nonstop from LA to Western Europe. She kept a suite year round at Claridge's in London, one of my favorite hotels.

She'd say things like, "Baby, I don't ever want you to work. You make the funny. I'll make the money."

In fairly short order, I realized that while she had no problem spending millions of Euros on horses, she'd never ever pick up a single dinner check (or anything else for that matter). She also always ordered like it was her last meal on death row. I was getting grumpy and broke with all of this false advertising.

I should mention that I asked we delay sex a bit, thinking we should get to know each other first. I figured what's the rush? Sex is always great and has never been a problem in the past. I'd never done this, but thought it might be worth a try. This was a mistake. Always have sex early. While sex isn't everything, it is the glue. Without glue, the whole structure falls in.

The day finally came, and while sex wasn't awful, it wasn't particularly inspired either. She was lazy and entitled, just like she was with her clothes on. That said, there's always room for improvement. We continued to try over the next few weeks.

For those of you who don't know, Nathan in Hebrew means "giver" and give I did.

In a vain attempt to defibrillate our soggy, Wonder Bread sex life, I serviced her so long and so masterfully (her words), she was nearly stuck to the ceiling when I finished. Exhausted, I rolled over onto my back, and gently placed my palm between her shoulder blades hoping for a little reciprocity (which hadn't yet happened in a half-dozen sleepovers).

OLIVIA: Uh, sweetheart. Just so you know. I don't do anything with the word "JOB" in it.

Outraged, I looked at my watch.

ME: Time of death: 11:39 p.m.

OLIVIA: Babe. Do you mean to tell me, you wouldn't date someone who doesn't suck dick?

ME: Babe. I mean to tell you, I wouldn't be *friends* with someone who doesn't suck dick.

"

Sid motioned me to sit back down and shouted back, "Get Johnny Williams on the phone!"

Chapter Thirty-Six

Johnny Williams

I met Sid Sheinberg through a friend shortly after moving to LA in 1994. That friend was kind enough to invite me over for Passover dinner as I couldn't afford a plane ticket home. I had an old Leica rangefinder camera loaded with black and white film. As a thank you, I sent some 8x10 prints of his grandkids seated at a piano lit by candles.

With those photos, he referred me to my first paid job as a photographer and later installed me as his CIO of his post MCA startup.

The stories are endless, but I'll share one.

I was sitting across from him at the end of the day in his office in the Hitchcock Bungalow on the Universal lot when Marsha, his longtime secretary with a big New York accent, shouted:

MARSHA: I have Spielberg!

I stood to give him some privacy and show myself out. Sid motioned me to sit back down and shouted back, "Get Johnny Williams on the phone!"

"Johnny" Williams was, of course, the legendary film composer John Williams, who had just won an Oscar for their latest film *Schindler's List*, which had also won best picture a day or two before.

The call connected and I gleefully listened to these three giants on a call.

JOHN WILLIAMS: Guys. We've done a lot of work together and I'm proud of it all, but this. This is my life's most important work and I thank you both.

SPIELBERG: You know… you weren't our first choice.

Dead silence for five seconds.

WILLIAMS: Um…

SHEINBERG: (Bellowing) It's true! Mozart wasn't available!

They all erupted with laughter like the big kids they were.

Sid Sheinberg was without peer the smartest man I've ever known. He was also the most charitable. Tough as nails with a heart of gold. Godspeed, Sidney. You made the world a better place.

"

"Oh. I just remembered, in the fridge over 'dere, 'dis bloke brung me some morphine suppositories. They're pretty good."

Chapter Thirty-Seven

Morphine Suppositories

1995, West Hollywood, California

A rock star friend invited me over to his house to hang out, catch up, and bang on some guitars.

KEITH: Hey, mate. Can I get you anything to drink?

ME: Yeah. Do you have any Scotch?

KEITH: Naw, mate. I got Rye.

ME: Anything else? Vodka? Tequila?

KEITH: Oh. I just remembered, in the fridge over 'dere, 'dis bloke brung me some morphine suppositories. They're pretty good.

ME: I don't know, man. I'm just not a lucky person.

KEITH: What does luck have to do wif' it?

ME: As much as I love a good opiate, I just don't want my parents to read in the newspaper that I was found dead of an overdose with my pants around my ankles, slumped over a sofa at a musician's house. They deserve better than that.

KEITH: Right then. Gin?

ME: Good.

"

Merv was a big personality,
white haired, whip smart,
incredibly charismatic,
charming, hilarious, and gay.

Chapter Thirty-Eight

Merv Griffin vs. the President of the United States

Years ago, I had to ditch a friend when I discovered he was a drug addict and stealing prescription pills from the homes of friends of mine.

Through LA's greatest job bank, Alcoholics Anonymous, he somehow landed a job as the personal assistant to Merv Griffin.

For those who don't know about Merv, he was an old-school tycoon in the truest sense of the word. Early on, he had a number one *Billboard* hit, "I've Got a Lovely Bunch of Coconuts." He hosted a popular talk show in the '70s, he created the number one and number two most successful TV shows of all time, *Wheel of Fortune* and *Jeopardy*. (He also wrote the music for both.) In addition, he owned a portfolio of hotels, resorts, and casinos. He kept his offices at his flagship LA property, The Beverly Hilton. Merv was a big personality, white haired, whip smart, incredibly charismatic, charming, hilarious, and gay.

His head of security and bodyguard was a guy called Al. Al was a fascinating cat who looked like a Scorsese mob character. Grey hair, curly fro, cop mustache, blue gradient shades. Grey suits. Pink shirts. Banker striped ties with double Windsor knots. Nickel-plated Colt 1911 in the waistband. No holster. Funny, smart, and a great storyteller.

He was a retired LAPD watch commander. He had killed many "assholes" in the line of duty. He was all business and he did not suffer fools gladly. We'd have lunch every few weeks, usually in the commissary at the hotel. We'd swap stories and laugh.

While the Beverly Hilton isn't the poshest hotel in Los Angeles, it does boast one unique feature —it has the largest ballroom in town. If you're doing a big show like The Golden Globes or any number of other things, it's the only game in town.

One day, the guys were walking back from lunch and decide to take a shortcut through the International Ballroom. Security was particularly high because they were setting up for the DNC event for President Clinton. The Secret Service were drilling holes, talking in earpieces, and doing Secret Service-y kinds of things.

SECRET SERVICE: Excuse me? Sir!

Al ignored them and kept walking.

SECRET SERVICE: SIR!

Al still couldn't be bothered.

Things were heating up now. There were now five guys following. Two ran ahead and cut Al off.

AL: What do YOU meter maids want?

SECRET SERVICE: Sir, United States Secret Service. Presidential detail. Why are you here?

AL: I'm Director of Security for this hotel and its owner, Mr. Griffin.

SECRET SERVICE: Sir. Are you carrying a weapon at this time?

AL: (Sneering) You're goddamned right I am.

SECRET SERVICE: Sir. I'm going to need your weapon.

AL: (Walking around them) Why don't you try and take it from me?

Things were getting tense and now maybe six guys were following. Al was a cool customer and calmly walked back into the offices of the Griffin Group. *All* the Secret Service agents followed into a small reception area.

Enter Merv Griffin.

MERV: Oooh. What the hell's going on here?

SECRET SERVICE: Sir, United States Secret Service. We work for the President. There can be no firearms on property while the President is here.

MERV: Oh noooo. That won't do at all. This man's job is to protect me.
I mean… Al, what the hell good are you without your gun?

Al folded his arms across his chest with a big FUCK YOU on his face.

SECRET SERVICE: Mr. Griffin. This isn't a negotiation. It's simply not
an option.

MERV: You're half right about that. (Merv to receptionist) The hotel
is closed. I'm going to need you to relocate all the guests. And you guys
need to tell the President he's going to have to find another venue for his
event tomorrow night. OR, I can. (Smiling) I have his cell number.

Game. Set. Match. Merv.

"

"What? Do you have shit in your ears? I asked if your balls sag?"

Chapter Thirty-Nine

Joan Rivers and My Balls

August 1, 2011

I did a shoot with Joan Rivers and appeared on her show. So smart. So funny. I had to stop shooting every few minutes because I was laughing so hard. Here's a snippet.

JOAN: Scott. How old are you?

ME: Legal.

JOAN: Shut the fuck up. How old are you?

ME: Cut me in half and count the rings.

JOAN: You asshole. How old?

ME: I'm 46.

JOAN: Do your balls sag?

ME: What?

JOAN: What? Do you have shit in your ears? I asked if your balls sag?

ME: Well, more than they did as a teenager... yeah.

JOAN: My vagina sags so much that when I got out of bed this morning in my hotel room, I stepped on it. It looked like I was wearing one of those grey fuzzy rabbit slippers.

* * *

PART TWO:

We were having breakfast in the morning while my crew was setting up.

JOAN: I've seen your work. It's very good, but it's not why I requested you.

ME: No?

JOAN: No. I heard you were funny and Jewish.

ME: I'm both.

JOAN: You don't look Jewish. How do I know you didn't lie to get the gig?

ME: Everyone named Nathan is either black or Jewish. I'm Jewish, but black from the waist down.

JOAN: I'm not so sure.

I stood up, unbuckled my belt, and started to unbutton my pants.

JOAN: OK, OK. I believe you! Put that thing away!

"

He slowly lowered his paper…
and with a furrowed brow said,
"What," with a hard emphasis
on the H sound.

Chapter Forty

Meeting Peter O'Toole

I met Peter O'Toole once at Gatwick airport when I was a teenager. He was reading the paper in an impeccable cream Savile Row suit, white shirt, and black tie, with a perfectly matched cashmere topcoat and hat on the seat next to him.

I was so awestruck by him, without thinking I shouted, "Hey, O'Toole!" He slowly lowered his paper, looked at me, and with a furrowed brow said, "What," with a hard emphasis on the H sound.

ME: What was it like?

HIM: (Impatient) What was WHAT like? (That H sound again)

ME: What was it like to be a nobody? An obscure British stage actor, then suddenly, overnight you're the biggest movie star in the world who just made the greatest film of all time that won all those Oscars.

HIM: (Smiling) Well, I did what any silly cunt would've done. I was in Los Angelees at the time and I bought the largest, whitest Rolls Royce a man could own and I drove down Sunset Boo-lee-vahd waving like the fucking Queen.

ME: Amazing. How was that?

HIM: No one gave a fuck.

His attention went back to his newspaper.

"

Getting Leo fresh off of Titanic was the ultimate get. It would be checkmate and kill every other Hughes project.

Chapter Forty-One

The Aviator

2002ish, West Hollywood, California

I'm at a regular client's production company for a few hours doing some IT work. I knew these guys for three years and they had yet to produce anything.

The CEO, who we'll call "Judas", was the type you get used to seeing around here. An East Coast trust fund kid with a prep school shag cut and clothes to match. Went to film school. Didn't have to work.

He had great taste in material, but for whatever the reason was never able to get anything going. He had one of those personalities that unintentionally seemed to offend people.

I was familiar with three books they were rights holders to. All great. All deserving of films, but all period pieces, which are costly to make.

ME: (to the two partners) What is your guys deal? These are all great stories. Why can't you get any of them made?

JUDAS: (irritated) Dude. Stay in your lane. You have no idea how difficult it is to get a film made.

ME: Let me ask you this. Is attaching a big bankable star enough to get a movie made?

JUDAS: Well, usually yeah

ME: If I can attach an A-lister to any of these, will you give me second position producer? I'm not getting fucked like I did on Malkovich.

JUDAS: (Rolling his eyes) Yeah. Deal.

The first book I read of his was *Howard Hughes: The Untold Story* by Peter Brown and Pat Broeske.

From childhood, I had admiration for Howard Hughes. He was more than a billionaire. He was a millionaire at 18. He devised the first drill bit to allow oil discovery through hard rock formations. He produced the costliest film ever made at the time. He set the world record for circumnavigating the globe via aircraft. He designed the worlds largest aircraft. He put the first satellite into space.

I was pre-sold on this project. My best friend at the time was the long-time girlfriend of Leo Di Caprio. Even though I saw this as a massive opportunity for everyone, I had to be careful. People are sensitive about their relationships. Rather than ask, I decided to take her temperature and began to tell her about how amazing Howard's life was.

As I got through the book incrementally, I would tell her more and more. She in turn began to tell Leo. He too became fascinated. It was time to make a move. I had Leo's phone number, but had never used it.

I was on Sunset Boulevard driving east through Beverly Hills. I called my then friend and told him I thought there was a chance we could get this done with Leo. He mentioned that there were several Hughes projects in development, so it was urgent we close this one quickly. I articulated the obvious. Getting Leo fresh off of *Titanic* was the ultimate get. It would be checkmate and kill every other Hughes project.

As we continued to discuss strategy, I saw out my windshield, on the western facing billboard of the 9000 Sunset building an ad for the movie *The People vs. Larry Flynt*.

I thought of a fib that ended up actually being true.

This second act of the story is via "Judas," some of which contradicts some of the various records out there. The truth is likely somewhere in between.

ME: Here's what we're doing. We're telling Leo, he has to commit now or it's going to go to Edward Norton and Milos Forman, the co-star and Director of *Flynt*.

Evidently Leo waffled a bit early in the conversation. "Yeah, call my manager Rick Yorn." Judas wasn't comfortable, but decided to try my

Hail Mary. It worked.

LEO: Edward Norton??? He's not Howard. He's a scrawny, ugly pussy who went to Yale. I'm Howard.

That was enough to get Leo who was in the neighborhood to drive straight to the Judas' office on Melrose Avenue.

They shook hands and began to chat. Judas asked Leo who he thought would be the right director. Leo didn't hesitate. He loved *The Insider* and liked the idea of Michael Mann. They called Mann. He came over. Mann explained that he was fully committed for the foreseeable future with *Ali* and *Collateral*. He did however insert himself as a producer in the project. Leo's second choice was Martin Scorsese as he had a great experience with him on *Gangs of New York*.

According to Judas, Michael Mann began acquiring rights to other Hughes projects in a rather piggish attempt to push Judas and I out. Things got really ugly, really fast. What the new producers didn't anticipate was the level of wealth Judas and his family possessed and could weather big litigation. I had no such ability.

Judas wasn't doing himself any favors either. He began sending a constant barrage of hectoring and harassing "creative" emails to Mann, Scorsese, et al. I was trying to control this loose cannon.

ME: What the fuck are you doing? Martin Scorsese and Michael Mann do not need your notes or help on this script. They've done this before. Back the fuck off. You got a massive film green lit. This is the time to focus and get your other projects off the ground.

JUDAS: No, Scott. They're ruining it.

ME: You're putting a gun in your mouth and asshole-ing yourself out of this project and the film business.

As I predicted, they stopped responding to him and he was banned from set. He ended up suing his way into 4th position producer and me? As per usual, I got nothing. I couldn't find a contingency lawyer willing to fight a fight this big. I was assed out.

I told Judas to never contact me again.

About a year after the films release, he reached out.

JUDAS: I'd like us to talk.

ME: There's nothing to talk about. We aren't friends Judas.

JUDAS: I'd like to make good on this.

ME: Fine. Send me half your producers fee.

JUDAS: I would like to give you some money.

He convinced me to come into the office. I didn't have the best attitude going into this meeting. I tried to convince myself to stay calm.

I walked into his office on the 8200 Block of Melrose Avenue. He stood to shake my hand. I put my hands in my pockets and sat down across from him.

The first thing I noticed was the framed Academy Award Nomination on the wall behind his desk. The second thing I saw was The Golden Globe statue on his desk for Best Picture.

ME: You should've put that Golden Globe in the drawer.

JUDAS: (Puzzled) Why would I do that?

ME: I'm not going to *do* it, but I have the overwhelming urge to smash your skull to pieces with it right now. I deserve it more than you do.

JUDAS: I know, but Scott, that's a little aggressive…

ME: What do you want, Judas?

JUDAS: I'd like to take you to lunch.

ME: What do you want?

He persisted, and had a reservation at Pané e Vino on Beverly Boulevard.

We sat down in a packed garden and he began to blubber.

JUDAS: I'm really sorry. This was a complicated deal…

ME: Are you really crying right now? Do you think this is a speeding ticket and you're the girl? Be a man. Stop crying. Have some dignity.

JUDAS: There's a lot you don't know. They fucked me. There was nothing I could do. There's a lot for us to discuss. There are a lot of questions.

ME: Questions? There's only ONE question here, Judas. Would *The Aviator* have been made without Scott Nathan? Yes or No?

Judas begins crying again...

JUDAS: No...

ME: People are staring. If you don't stop crying, I'm leaving. Do you have a check for me or not?

JUDAS: Yes. I'll write you one back at the office.

We get through lunch and go back to the office. He tells me he's giving me $10,000 as a finders fee. I tell him I know what his producers fee is and this is an outrageously low offer. Then he tells me, he'll have to pay me in installments of $1000.00 a month for 10 months. I was in no position to negotiate, so I took it. He never asked me to sign anything, but here we are.

Months later he called me.

JUDAS: So, I still feel bad.

The balls on this guy.

ME: Good. You should.

JUDAS: I have a new documentary coming out and I've given you an associate producer credit on it.

ME: Are you kidding me? I don't want it. I don't know anything about this movie. I hate fake credits. I had nothing to do with it. Take my name off.

JUDAS: It's too late. Everything's been printed.

I hung up.

It's my sole producing credit on **IMDB**. Pretty sure no one saw the movie.

"

"You need to shoot me or pay me, but you can't keep sleeping with me for free."

Chapter Forty-Two

Bed Conversation with a Model

2008

HER: Can I be honest about something?

ME: Sure.

HER: You need to shoot me or pay me, but you can't keep sleeping with me for free.

ME: Your honesty is oddly... refreshing. I'll get back to you.

HER: I'm probably the hottest girl you've ever been with.

ME: Top 200 for sure.

HER: You're an asshole.

ME: I thought we were being honest.

66

"Let me know the next time you're in LA. We can grab a lunch or drinks." That's when things took a turn for the worse.

Chapter Forty-Three

My Meeting at Rolling Stone

I was in New York City on a shoot and decided to make the rounds and take a few meetings. It was a boyhood dream to someday shoot for *Rolling Stone* magazine. This was in the days when Annie Leibovitz was shooting creative, colorful high-concept stories. *Rolling Stone* at the time was one of the great chroniclers of American culture in any medium.

Portfolio reviews are typically less than 15 minutes. They flip through your big, heavy, leather-bound book, then off you go. After an hour or so, the photo editor and I shook hands, looking forward to our next chat. As we stood, I said, "Let me know the next time you're in LA. We can grab a lunch or drinks." That's when things took a turn for the worse.

HER: I never go to the LA shoots.

ME: Too busy to travel that far?

HER: No. LA is the single most disgusting, vile place I've ever been in my entire life.

ME: Curious. What's the second most disgusting place you've ever been?

HER: Mumbai, India.

ME: Hmm… y'know… on my way into this meeting I saw a naked man. Right down there on 6th Avenue, taking a shit on the sidewalk.

HER: (Mad face) This conversation is over.

ME: Good talk.

She never booked me, but I stand by that joke.

“

The first thing I noticed about the mansion was what a faded dame she was… the definition of "deferred maintenance."

Chapter Forty-Four

The Playboy Mansion

Summer, 1999

I was out one night with a modeling agent friend and about a dozen of her models. We were at the hotspot du jour, a large nightclub called Las Palmas on a street with the same name in Hollywood. We were at a long rectangular table. I noticed out of the corner of my eye, Hugh Hefner was eyeing our group.

If I've learned anything about this town, it's that no one feeds the hungry. The only palms that ever get greased are the ones who don't need it, so I made it a point to not notice Hef, the Bentley twins, or his two guy friends. I didn't need to tell the models, since they were all too young to know who he was anyway.

After an hour or so, one of Hef's friends approached me. The only man at the table to introduce himself and to invite us to the Playboy Mansion. I'm not going to lie, but this was a boyhood fantasy. In my childhood, we all grew up on pilfered *Playboy* magazines. It wasn't just the naked women, but the lifestyle that we yearned for.

I feigned indifference.

DR. MARK: I'd like to invite you all to the mansion for our party tomorrow night. Come early. Stay as long as you like.

ME: Hey, it's nice to meet you, Doc. Ladies? Would you like to go?

Models are well used to swatting away old men, and these thoroughbreds had all seen the mountaintop. Despite their youth, they'd seen and done it all already. They'd shot all the campaigns, walked all the catwalks and didn't know what the Playboy Mansion was, and didn't much care. Models. Real models aren't impressed. It's part of their charm. I took his business card and told him I'd call him the next day.

I called him the next day with a guest list of me +4 guests. We arrived a few hours before the party started, had cocktails and sat around the pool.

The first thing I noticed about the mansion was what a faded dame she was. This place I'd seen endless photos of growing up, was the definition of "deferred maintenance." The furniture was worn out. The paint yellowed. The foyer smelled like dog piss, and the pool furniture was faded and stained. The exercise equipment in the gym was Nautilus brand from the early '80s and beige. The zoo was pretty cool. Flamingoes and Peacocks roamed the vast lawns and the zookeepers wore the requisite khakis, but with black Playboy Bunny shoulder patches.

As night fell, the crowd began to grow. By 10 p.m. it was the bacchanal we signed up for. Stars, nudity and revelry.

Being the vocal and gregarious guy *I* am, I began to socialize. First with a small group of guys and girls at the bar, while waiting for my next cocktail. I'm not five minutes in when a Playboy security guy rolled up on me. He was bald with a G. Gordon Liddy, push broom mustache, a tan suit with a white shirt. "Sir, I'm with security. These ladies are with Mr. Hefner and you can't speak to them." The girls were embarrassed and rolled their eyes. I apologized and excused myself. I moved to the chaise lounges by the pool to the left of the entrance to the fabled grotto, where I'd run into a couple of friends who were with other guests.

Same security goon shows up again with the same line. Oh, fuck this. I don't bother anyone. I don't hit on anyone. Pissed, I excused myself again and began to walk the property. I spied a small building that looked like guesthouse to the south of the driveway. The door was open and I showed myself in.

It was "The Game House." Like the rest of the place, it was worn and shabby. There were two or three pinball machines and some ancient video games like Ms. Pacman and Galaga or Asteroids. There were also two bedrooms. One was all mirrors. Walls and ceilings with no bed, dirty greige carpeting with an unusually thick layer of padding. I later learned it was called "The Orgy Room." The other room had a bed. A weird nautical bed like you'd find in a '70s sailboat with navy sheets.

I started a game of pinball on the *Playboy* themed pinball machine and thought about how I was going to navigate this party without getting thrown out.

Three sassy blondes walked in, and struck up a conversation with me. Bitter, I said "I'm not sure if I'm allowed to talk to you. I keep getting in trouble for talking to people." They were first timers too. When I asked what they did, they said "We surf" and were visiting from Orange County.

We were laughing and having our own mini party when finally one of them asked.

CORA: Hey! Have you ever taken ecstasy before?

ME: Yes. Once (laughing). Didn't end well.

The three blondes were intrigued.

ME: I went to a black tie event in Chicago with three girls I grew up with. Like *friend* friends. We all ended up taking a bath together. Didn't fool around or anything, but got super weird washing each others hair and bodies. None of us could make eye contact the next day at brunch.

I guess I still had some midwestern innocence back at the turn of the century.

JO: Shut up and take these!

Without pause, I swallowed the two pink pills. Without going into too much detail, my first threesome was a foursome. We stayed until the next afternoon, and only left the game house once and that was for food and booze.

We continued this back at my place, when I met my new female next-door neighbor Pauline peeping in on us all having sex on the sofa.

I didn't really care and thought I'd embarrass her a little:

ME: Hey! What're you doing, you peeper!

PAULINE: I'm so sorry, I wanted to stop watching, but I couldn't.

ME: All good.

We're dear friends to this day. I introduce her as "Pauline the Peeper."

"

Lesson: Don't pretend to be proficient in a language that you aren't.

Chapter Forty-Five

When In Rome

I was in Rome in Piazza Farnese after a fashion business event with an Italian model, two editors, and two legendary designers. I was the only American.

Lesson: Don't pretend to be proficient in a language that you aren't.

ITALIAN GIRL: *Amore*, do you need help with the menu?

ME: Um. No. I took three semesters of Italian in College. I think I can handle ordering dinner.

We finished and one of the designer guys complimented my meal choice.

HIM: Eh, Scott, that was a very adventurous order for an American.

ME: You think? What was so adventurous?

HIM: Tell me what you theenk you order.

ME: (In what I believed to be a perfect Roman accent) *Bistecca di Cavallino Tartufo Bianco.*

HIM: And thees ees?

ME: Steak with white truffles.

HIM: Eh… you meess a word.

ME: Doesn't Cavallino mean "with white truffles"?

HIM: (Laughing) Eh. No. Eeta means a *baby horse.*

“

What do I know about slavery?
I'm a Jew from the suburbs…
I've never dated a slave
trader before.

Chapter Forty-Six

My Girlfriend, the Slave Trader

Spring, 2006

I was taking a Wednesday off to play golf with a friend at Brentwood Country Club in Los Angeles.

My longtime girlfriend at the time was delightfully antithetical to LA. A sweet girl from Virginia. Natural, almost hippie ashy blonde with sparkly green eyes. Age appropriate. Mayflower type. Creative, talented, and never discussed boring celebrity gossip.

When you're in a relationship in LA you have two huge payoffs. Built-in dinner plans and someone to keep you company while sitting in soul-crushing traffic.

She was at work and we were chatting away on this beautiful morning. I pulled up to the white, wooden gatehouse at the club, in my white shoes, white trousers, and white cricket sweater.

ME: Hey, babe. I'm pulling up to the gate. Hang on for a sec.

GF: OK, babe.

GUARD: Morning, sir. May I have the member's name you're playing with today?

ME: I'm playing with Mr. Brown.

This guard was old. African American. Eighties with a snow-white beard. As I was looking him over, gold buttons, brocade like a Park Avenue doorman, I also noticed he had the same last name as my girlfriend.

ME: Baby, you're not going to believe this! This gentleman here at the club has the same last name as you.

GF: Oh, my God. Is he black?

At the EXACT SAME TIME, the guard asked:

GUARD: She white?

GF: Baby. Stop talking. Please. Don't say another word and just drive through.

ME: Wait? What? I mean, don't you think that's amazing? (To guard) What are the chances that you and my girlfriend have the same last name?

GF: Seriously, Scott, I'm begging you. You need to stop talking *right now*.

The guard was fuming. I was confused.

Gate opened and as I was pulling up to the valet/bag drop…

GF: Seriously. What is wrong with you?

ME: I don't understand. What did I do?

GF: You know I'm from Virginia.

ME: Yes…

GF: You know my family grew tobacco.

ME: (Still not getting it) Umm. Yeah?

GF: Scott. I'm not proud of this, but if he's black and we have the same name, it means my family owned his family. How did you not connect these dots?

ME: What do I know about slavery? I'm a Jew from the suburbs and you'll have to forgive me, but I've never dated a slave trader before.

GF: Ugh. Have a good game. I'll see you at the restaurant at eight.

ME: K. Love you.

66

I've never had any secrets. Why start now? My superpower is not giving a fuck.

Chapter Forty-Seven

Pandemic Porn

March, 2020

At the start of the coronavirus pandemic, the world had become a different place. Six continents had just shut down. I, like millions of others around the world, was burning money with little savings and was trying to think of some way, any way, to keep the lights on and food in the fridge.

Now, I had been training at social distancing for a long time. I'm quite certain that were it an Olympic event (and held in summer), I could take at least Silver. I've been more or less living like Howard Hughes without the jars of urine (or money) since 2011.

One afternoon I was catching up with adult film star Ivy Wolfe. Ivy and I met through mutual friend Sam Phillips, a veteran radio personality and now an editor at *Penthouse* magazine. Coincidentally, a few months after we met, I was booked by *Penthouse* to shoot her cover and Pet story.

I did it under a pseudonym, because I was worried about my advertising and fine art career. But later I decided, fuck it. I've never had any secrets. Why start now? My superpower is not giving a fuck. I've been watching porn since I was 10 years old and stole my dad's Betamax tapes of *Deep Throat* and *Behind the Green Door*. This generation similarly learned about sex from PornHub. Fortunately all millennials and Gen-Zers have been programmed to believe anal is second base. This is perhaps their most redeeming feature.

We're all dead soon anyway, and that's a fact.

Ivy and I were talking about how we were dealing with the pandemic. And how neither of us could work. I had just done my first Zoom video conference meeting.

ME: What if we could create a series, a new genre of porn, centered around social distancing.

IVY: What would that look like?

ME: I'm not sure. You're an A-lister. What if we wrangled a few big stars, invited them to a video conference, and you all had virtual sex? We'll then all sell it on pay per view on OnlyFans.

IVY: Sounds fun. If you organize and cast it, I'll be there.

Our first episode was a four-girl lesbian orgy. Each one of them at home with their ring lights and webcams. It got press in dozens of outlets around the world reaching tens of millions of people. The press was no accident. I learned how to be my own publicist through a woman I briefly dated who worked in White House Comms under Obama. She imparted some simple principles. To name a few:

1. Journalists are inherently lazy people. Write the story *with* the headline *as* the press release.

2. Never make it about your product. If you do, no one will help. Create a tailor-made story that gets easily approved by their editor and gets them paid. The pitch to the *Wall Street Journal* is different than the pitch to *Esquire*. At the very least, the headline and writing style is different.

3. Look up journalists that have written about anything in your space before, then find them, stalk them and pitch them.

Headlines varied from writer to writer, but the gist was "How the adult film industry is not only surviving, but thriving during the quarantine." The pitch was interesting, clickable, and not too dirty. It opened us to many media outlets. I pitched a dozen writers. I got four stories that got picked up by news aggregators around the world and reached than millions of readers.

They did well. All the performers were bored and basically did us a favor, but all made tens of thousands of dollars for 40 minutes of work.

66

He was a legendary big hitter, big steroid abuser and an unapologetically massive prick in interviews. This will be fun.

Chapter Forty-Eight

The Slugger

2014, Pebble Beach Golf Links, Monterey County, California

I'm once again fulfilling my duties as America's Guest (A.G.), a term for a guy who frequently plays golf at other people's country clubs, but doesn't actually belong to one.

This trip was a two day charity tournament in partnership with Major League Baseball. I grew up going to Bulls and Blackhawks games, but never followed baseball much.

The setup for pairings was by lottery. The first day I was paired with a right fielder for the Angels. Nice guy. Hit it far.

That evening there was a fancy dinner with balls all over the tables to collect autographs, charity auctions and so on. At dessert time, they announced the pairings for the following day. The guy I got, even I had heard of. We'll call him Chuck. He was a legendary big hitter, big steroid abuser and an unapologetically massive prick in interviews. This will be fun. I love these kinds of people, and tend to get along with them.

Before the dinner is over, my friends are endlessly harassing me to switch players with them. I told them all no.

BRUCE: C'mon. Switch with me. You don't even like baseball.

ME: No, but I like characters.

BRUCE: He's supposed to be an asshole.

ME: I'll take my chances.

We step onto the first tee at Pebble and I'm marveling at the sheer enormity of this guy.

While Pebble Beach is one of the world's most famous golf courses, it has *the* worst first tee in golf. You're teeing off in what is essentially an outrageously overpriced strip mall where everyone's yapping and watching you hit, and everyone there looks like Lindsey Graham with food poisoning. It's a somewhat tricky left to right shot. A high draw for a lefty like me. This is a hole where you want to just get into play on the short grass and GTFO out of the mall. Pebble isn't terribly long or punitive, but it's greens are barely larger than beach towels and the rough is merciless, should you miss the short grass.

I smoothed a playable, but not super long 3-wood onto the left center of the fairway. Safe. My partner, the legend proceeds to nuke one well over 300 yards, but it's through the fairway and in deep shit. I'm considerate and try in vain to help him find his ball. We don't find it. We continue playing with little chitchat. We're both focused on playing well. We're both playing like the mid handicappers we are.

We're standing on the hole number six tee box. One of the best par fives and no doubt one of the best views on the course. It's the first hole that reveals Stillwater Cove in all of her majesty. It's also the hole where Tiger Woods hit one of his best shots ever: a 205-yard seven iron from ankle deep rough to help him cruise to a 15 shot victory in the 2000 U.S. Open.

It's Chuck's turn to hit. He looks back at me and says:

CHUCK: Scott man. I've gotta tell you. You're the best amateur I've ever played with.

ME: (Laughing) Oh Fuck off. Don't make fun of me. I'm not playing well.

CHUCK: Oh, that's not what I meant. I mean you're cool cause you haven't asked me one baseball question all day!

ME: Oh, Chuck. I'm your guy. I don't give a fuck about baseball.

Chuck smiles, looks me dead in the eye and presents a boulder sized fist to bump.

CHUCK: Me either.

We get back to the clubhouse laughing and slapping each others backs.

"

There's not just a pile of dog shit. There are more piles of dog shit than there is floorspace.

Chapter Forty-Nine

The Child Star

Spring, 2014

There's a wardrobe stylist I had been working with for years we'll call Elizabeth. She was talented and had good, positive set vibes. We were at Milk Studios in Hollywood on a three-day fashion advertising shoot. We were between shots and chit chatting. She was from a big LA family and frequently spoke of her brothers and sisters. I had never asked her about them before.

ME: How many siblings do you have?

ELIZABETH: Seven. Four brothers and three sisters.

ME: Tell me about them.

When she got to the last one, it was a child actor who had found success in her 20s and 30s. I had had a bit of a celebrity crush on her in my 20s.

ME: I didn't realize that was your sister.

ELIZABETH: Oh. Yeah.

ME: Let's shoot her sometime.

Elizabeth had this uncomfortable look on her face. Like I had crossed a line or something. Her expression said, "Eh… Yeah. No."

Being an insecure person, I immediately thought "What? I'm good enough to book you all the time and make you tens of thousands of dollars, but not good enough to shoot your sister?" I left it alone, but it pissed me off. I'd shot dozens of bigger stars than her sister.

When that campaign dropped, everyone on the team began posting the photos of the print ads and billboards on our socials. A day or two later, I received a Facebook message from the actress sister.

ASHLEY: Hello, my name is Ashley, and I'm Elizabeth's sister. I love your work and wanted to ask if you'd like to shoot sometime.

ME: Thanks! I dig your work too. Let's grab lunch and hatch a plan.

We met a few days later at Cheebo, on the corner of Sunset and Sierra Bonita in Hollywood. We get along super well. She's quick witted, sexy and funny. Just before I ask for the bill, she catches me looking at my watch.

ASHLEY: (grinning) Hey. You got a date?

ME: Huh, no.

ASHLEY: You're checking your watch. Do you have someplace to be?

ME: Oh, yeah. I'm actually going to meet a couple of guy friends at the gun club to shoot clays.

ASHLEY: I want to shoot clays!

ME: Come with. Have you ever done it before?

ASHLEY: No, but I'm good at everything.

Cocky. I kind of like it.

We arrive at Oak Tree Gun Club in Newhall early and I decide to take her onto a Trap field first, since it's the most forgiving of the clay disciplines and put a 20 gauge Belgium Browning Superposed in her hands. It's lighter and easier to shoot for smaller people than a 12 gauge.

I gave her instructions on how to safely handle the gun. Loading and unloading, hold point and break point. Then I smoke five or six targets, so she gets the rhythm of the game. I take the remote control into my hands and hand Ashley the gun.

She was right. She is good at everything. I've never seen anything like it before, but she smashed 22 out of 25 targets on the first try. We then joined my friends and moved over to a Skeet field for the rest where she also did shockingly well.

We're driving back, and I exit the Ventura Freeway at Hollywood and Highland to drop her off at her car near the restaurant. We're on

Franklin Avenue. She points up the hill and says "Have you ever been there before?"

ME: The Magic Castle?

ASHLEY: Yes.

ME: Yeah. A handful of times.

ASHLEY: I love magic.

ME: Me too. They're so good there.

ASHLEY: Hey, I'm not quite ready to call it a day yet. Do you want to go someplace and watch the sunset?

Is this turning into a date?

We drive to Soho House West Hollywood on Sunset Boulevard which sits atop a mid-rise building with spectacular 360 degree views of the city.

As we're checking in with reception, the lady at the front desk asks:

ANNE: Hey Scott! Are you here for Magic Castle night?

Ashley and I look at each other, confused.

ME: Tell me about it.

ANNE: It's a new regular thing we'll be doing. We get the best magicians from the Castle and have a show in the screening room.

Ashley and I look at each other. Kismet. Destiny?

ME: I never remember to RSVP to the special events here in time and always miss them.

ANNE: Come down in 45 minutes, 15 minutes before it starts and I'll sneak you in first.

Ashley and I sat on the penthouse terrace and watched the sunset. I had a glass of rosé. She abstained. We shared French fries before heading down to the screening room. I ask if it's ok that we sit down in front so we get picked for magic tricks. She's all about it.

The next people let in were Jaime King and her then husband Kyle. They were seated to our immediate right. She and Ashley knew each other and had worked together in the past.

ASHLEY: You guys, I'm gonna go pee so I don't miss the show.

Ashley heads out and Jaime turns to me.

JAIME: So, how did you two meet?

I don't know why I do stuff like this, but sometimes it just slips out of my mouth.

ME: Craigslist.

JAIME: *You* met *her* on Craigslist?

ME: Yes. There's this section called "Casual Encounters." And, what it is, is...

JAIME: I *know* what it is! Um, who's the member here?

ME: I am.

Jaime looks understandably sketched out.

My plan all along was to say "Just kidding," but before I knew it, a friend behind me tapped my shoulder to say hi and then a friend of hers called her away and I'm panicked. I have to tell her I was kidding before Ashley gets back. My head is swiveling back and forth between Jaime and the people I was talking to.

I'm too late.

Ashley plops back down between us, and before I could say anything:

JAIME: Hey, so Scott here tells me you two met on Craigslist...

ASHLEY: Yes. Casual Encounters.

Is she my soulmate? Who else thinks like me? The magic show went well and we kissed goodnight.

We had a couple more dates and did some sex on the third. Things were going well. My bias against actors was fading. She was brilliant, funny and a real artist. Eccentric and mouthy to be sure, but I liked her. Finally, I pulled the trigger and posted a pic of us. Her sister called a few hours later.

ELIZABETH: Hey. Saw you hung out with Ash.

ME: Yeah. She's great.

ELIZABETH: Do me a favor. Please don't let her anywhere near alcohol.

ME: I'm not much of a drinker and she hasn't had any in the times we've hung out.

I could hear some impatience in her voice. Maybe she was annoyed I went out with her sister without telling her, but, Ashley contacted me and we're all grownups here.

This was the last moment of peace there would be with Ashley.

The following day:

ASHLEY: Hey. I keep coming over to your side of town. I want you to come west, see my house and take me to lunch.

We make plans. I'll come to her house on the Westside and we plan to drive to Malibu for lunch.

I arrived at her house at 11 a.m. in Mar Vista, or Playa Del Rey or one of those other West LA, no man's land, nondescript areas that I only go to for meetings at ad agencies.

It's a cute bungalow. White, wooden, with a deep green front door, green roof shingles and a white picket fence. The door is open and the screen door closed. Duran Duran (whom I loathe) is playing. I ring the bell. Ashley shouts "Come in!" from another room. I enter the second-grossest thing I've ever seen since the bog scene in *Trainspotting*.

I survey the space and am in utter shock. There's not just a pile of dog shit. There are more piles of dog shit than there is floorspace. It's a visual and olfactory assault. Easily 40–50 piles of shit, puddles of piss and other detritus. There are also crumpled Bud Light cans everywhere, dirty clothes, towels and dog hair. Heaps of it. Ashley enters the living room. She's wearing a denim dress that's not only on backwards, but also inside out. Her tits and the tag are out. She looks rough. Visibly stumbling drunk and slurring, holding a beer. When I'm uncomfortable, I joke:

ME: Oh, is it happy hour already?

ASHLEY: I. Am. Shitfaced.

ME: How many of those beers have you had?

ASHLEY: 54.

ME: That's impossible. No one can drink 54 beers. Even if you could, there's no way you could also keep count.

ASHLEY: (Still slurring and stumbling) What're you, fucking stupid?

All the joy and hope I had for her is draining out of me.

ME: Yeah. Common knowledge. Ask anyone.

ASHLEY: Pointing to a pile of beer cans and cartons. What do you see over there?

ME: A whole lot of empty beer cans.

ASHLEY: No dummy. What you see is three 18-packs… and (raising her can) this is my last beer.

I'm doing math in my head… carry the one…

ME: Ah. That *does* equal 54! Listen, I think I'm gonna go.

ASHLEY: You said you were going to take me to lunch at the beach and we're fucking going.

ME: You're in no condition to go anywhere. I'll talk to you later.

I'm deflated. I'm heartbroken. Once again, my dreams were dashed. I feel like crying. I got into the car and she sneaks in the passenger side. I'm at a loss for what to do. I don't want conflict. I don't want to kick her out of my car. I start driving, hoping she'll sober up by the time we make it to Malibu in Saturday traffic. I take the long way.

I had made a reservation at Nobu, but didn't tell her. There's no way we're going anywhere we're guaranteed to know at least ten people there. I park the car on Pacific Coast Highway. I decide we'll eat at The Farm, a restaurant at the end of Malibu Pier. She's loud, belligerent, and I've been over this since we left the house. We step onto the pier and she asks if she can try on my hat. This hat is one of the few things I'm precious about. I'd loan someone my car or motorcycle before this hat. It was handmade from a beaver pelt, took months to make and cost more than several vehicles I've owned.

ME: No. It's too windy and will blow off your head.

I have a massive head. Like Carly Simon, Mick Jagger, Leo DiCaprio big. It barely fits through doorways. Ashley jumps up laughing and grabs it off my head, puts it on her head, then violently pulls on the sides of the stiff brim, nearly breaking it. I'm not having fun. Not 10 seconds go by before the wind grabs it and flings it into the ocean. I hate her.

ME: I hate you right now.

ASHLEY: (climbing onto the pier fence) I'll jump off and get it.

I should have let her, but it's at least a 40-foot drop into rough water.

ME: If you jump off this pier, you will die.

ASHLEY: If you don't let me jump, you aren't allowed to be angry about me losing it.

ME: The hell I can't.

She has no idea how angry I can get. I wanted to leave, but I was hungry. I motion to the hotel next door, The Malibu Beach Inn. It didn't require driving and parking again. We enter, and head for the restaurant on a deck overlooking the ocean and approach the hostess. Ashley is zero percent quieter or less obnoxious.

ASHLEY: Hello! We'd like THAT table (pointing to a round six-top on the edge of the deck.)

HOSTESS: I'm afraid that table is reserved for a party of six, but I can seat you inside if that's OK.

ASHLEY: Yeah, whatever. We're sitting there.

Fucking actors. Ashley walks past her and sits down at the 6-top. I look at the hostess with sympathetic eyes. She says nothing and does nothing. I walk over to the table, but don't sit.

ME: I'm going to the restroom. Please don't order any alcohol.

ASHLEY: (screaming) Excuse me! I'd like a Ketel One Martini dirty. Three olives!

I should never have gone back for her.

I return from the restroom to face a man in a well-tailored suit with his arms folded across his chest. He looks pissed.

HOTEL MANAGER: Are you with *her?*

ME: Yes. I'm sorry.

HOTEL MANAGER: Get out of my hotel. Now.

ME: What happened?

HOTEL MANAGER: *Get. The FUCK. Out of my hotel.*

Great.

We leave and I set my GPS to the shortest route to her house and get rid of this liability. She's so drunk, she falls out of my SUV on arrival. She's so sloppy, I figure I should walk her in, lock the door behind me and let her sleep it off.

As we enter her living room, she trips and falls face first onto a cast iron and glass cocktail table. Her chin is split open and blood is pouring out. I run to the bathroom, but there are no clean towels. I find a dirty, dog hair covered one on her bedroom floor. It's white and quickly became saturated with blood. She needs a hospital.

ME: Nine-point-six for the blown dismount. OK, stupid. We're going to St. Johns.

ASHLEY: We are NOT going to the HOSPITAL! I don't DO bureaucracy.

ME: You have no brain and you need stitches.

ASHLEY: Absolutely not. I'll Krazy Glue that shit.

She stumbles to the kitchen, pulls out a blue plastic toolbox from underneath the sink, produces a tube of Krazy Glue and begins putting glue into her chin gash. I didn't know what to do. She ended up naked somewhere along the way. I wanted to run, but unsure if I should.

I pause, looking at her, wondering how she got here. She's on a filthy brown velour sofa, nude and holding a blood and glue soaked towel to her face.

Over her right shoulder, I noticed a yellowed framed page from *Daily Variety*. It was an ad for The Academy of Motion Picture Arts and Sciences members. A production still of a from a movie she starred in many years ago: "For your Consideration. Best Actress."

Reflexively, I took out my camera and shot a photo of this whole scene. The nude, battered drunk in squalor and the bloody towel contrasting with her former glory. I'm a photographer. I see moments like this.

Hours later, it felt too gross and predatory for even taking it and deleted the photo.

We didn't speak for a few weeks, when out of the blue, she called.

ASHLEY: Babe. There are some things I need to tell you. I'm super ashamed. I have bipolar disorder and stopped taking my meds, which led to me self-medicating with alcohol. I haven't drank since I saw you and would love another chance to make it right with you.

ME: I appreciate your sharing this with me. I also think rehab may be in order.

ASHLEY: I know, but I can't afford $40,000 a month for rehab.

After some back and forth…

ME: If I were to get you a bed for free in a top rehab, would you go?

ASHLEY: Yes.

ME: I'll get back to you.

My next call was to my pal Drew "Dr. Drew" Pinsky, who has always been there for me. I explained who she was, what the situation was and that there was no way she could be going through recovery on national television.

DR. DREW: Scott. It doesn't have to be now, but one of these days we need to have a talk about the women you choose to date.

ME: Drew, I know. It's not lost on me.

He agrees to work on it for me. A few hours later, he calls.

DR. DREW: OK. I found her a bed for 28 days of treatment at a great facility in Boca Raton, Florida. Can you get her there by Friday?

ME: Yes. Let me work on it.

My next call was to her sister. She wasn't pleased with any of this.

ME: She's in terrible shape and needs to go to rehab. I got her a bed in Boca. Will you split a full fare ticket to Palm Beach with me?

ELIZABETH: Scott. No matter what she tells you, she will never, ever go.

ME: I just spoke to her. She's agreed to go.

ELIZABETH: Scott. We've been going through this since high school. She won't go. Also, why are you involved in this?

ME: I'm involved because I care about her and we've become close.

ELIZABETH: What do you mean "close"?

ME: We've been dating.

ELIZABETH: (Irritated) What on earth would lead you to believe that you're dating my sister?

ME: Um. Talking five times a day. Sleeping in the same bed a few nights a week.

ELIZABETH: That *is* dating. I had no idea. You know she has a longtime boyfriend, right?

ME: No. I don't see how that's even possible. Who is he?

ELIZABETH: It's her old college professor, Brian.

I feel so stupid. My plan is to do my Mitzvah and move on.

I call Ashley back and tell her I got her the bed. I don't mention the boyfriend. I want this behind me.

ASHLEY: Oh, babe. I can't go. I just booked a three-episode arc on my friend's network procedural. I start the day after tomorrow. Also, my call time is 4:45 a.m. and I'm going to need you to pick me up and drive me to the Sony lot.

We argued back and forth about her need for treatment. Her sister was right, though.

ME: Uh, no. You can take an Uber.

ASHLEY: (Enraged bratty actress) You WILL wake up at 3 a.m. and drive me or there is no us. I don't know how to use apps and I don't DO bureaucracy. (Yeah, that again).

ME: Then take a taxi or ask the producers to send a P.A. or a car service to pick you up because I'm not.

ASHLEY: None of that is happening! You WILL pick me up, or you will never see this pussy again.

ME: If I'm honest, I wasn't planning on it anyway. Why don't you have Brian drive you?

Silence hung in the air for at least five seconds.

ASHLEY: What???

ME: Yeah. Your boyfriend you neglected to tell me about.

ASHLEY: Who told you about Brian?

ME: (With no fucks left to give.) Your sister threw you under the bus. You're a bad person.

I didn't ever expect to hear back from Ashley but, alas, I did the next evening at 8:30 p.m. She was cycling manic:

ASHLEY: Babe, you would've been so proud of me. My scenes were amazing. I had the longest monologue, and nailed it so perfectly I got a standing ovation from the cast and crew.

Seeing no value in any more confrontation...

ME: I am proud of you. That's amazing. Congratulations.

We chatted for a while longer, and by chatting, I mean I listened to her ramble for 15 minutes or so.

ASHLEY: OK. I have the same super early call time and need to learn my lines. Call you after wrap.

I didn't hear from Ashley all day and most of the evening. She finally called at 9:30.

ME: Hey! How did it go?

For the first 10 seconds, all I heard was crying, wailing and screaming. No bueno.

ME: Uh. Hello?

ASHLEY: OK, so I was so amped up last night that I couldn't fall asleep. I tried and tried and didn't know what to do, so I had a beer.

ME: By a beer, do you mean you drank an entire brewery again?

ASHLEY: Well, I must have. All I can remember is that I was in no condition to drive to the Sony lot, so I called production and asked if someone could pick me up. They were not happy, but they sent someone. I tried to pull it together, but they quickly realized I was also in no condition to work, and the producers started screaming at me. They were so rude.

ME: Oh, God. Then what?

This set her off, which wasn't difficult.

ASHLEY: Then what??? *Then what???* Then they fired me and told me they're suing me for $165,000 for the cost of the shoot day or whatever.

For lack of a better adjective, this was becoming tiresome and a situation I should've dipped out of weeks earlier. I knew it would probably anger her, but I let it fly.

ME: *Now* have you hit rock bottom? *Now* will you go to rehab and stop trying to do this on your own?

She was hysterical and weeping. She said she would figure out her schedule and get back to me.

I never heard from her again.

"

Well, does he use a machine?
Does he facilitate the sex
with a mare by playing
Barry White records?

Chapter Fifty

The Golden Cock

Winter, 2014

I'm dating this hedge fund manager. She's obsessed with horses, which is annoying. I love animals, but only *like* horses. She talks about them ad infinitum. It's mind numbing, but there's nothing wrong with individualizing and having our own interests outside of the relationship. I don't need someone I'm dating to be interested in watches, English motorcycles or Edwardian shotguns.

One morning, in a show of support I attend one of her horse shows. It's out in Santa Ynez. It's hot, sunny, dusty and boring. I'll never understand people who like to watch horses basically go around and around in circles in cosplay. Then again, I'll never understand men who watch football and yell at televisions either.

I decide to step outside and smoke. A tanned, handsome, older grey haired gentleman pulls up in a contemporary Aston Martin convertible finished in British Racing Green.

DOCTOR: Hey. You're new.

ME: Hi, yes. Where are all the guys?

DOCTOR: (laughing) Oh, you really *are* new! Listen. I don't know who your girlfriend is, but let me tell you something. She will never love you the way she loves her horses.

ME: I figured that one out on the first date. So you guys *never* come to these things?

DOCTOR: (laughing) No! We pay for all of it. We go to *none* of it.

So, after the show, she's walking me around the arena and barn and begins introducing me to people: various owners, riders, breeders and trainers. We stop at this shorter Mexican guy who had a real sweetness about him.

OLIVIA: Scott, this is Octavio.

ME: (Shaking hands) *Mucho gusto*, Octavio.

We keep walking.

ME: What does Octavio do? Is he a trainer?

OLIVIA: No. He's the Collector.

ME: What's a Collector?

OLIVIA: He harvests the sperm from my stud stallions for breeding.

ME: So, Octavio jerks horses off for a living?

OLIVIA: Why must you always find a way to make everything gross?

I shrug.

ME: Well, does he use a machine? Does he facilitate the sex with a mare by playing Barry White records?

OLIVIA: No, he uses his hands.

ME: So Octavio literally jerks horses off for a living?

OLIVIA: Ugh. Yes.

ME: Well, he did have very soft hands.

Olivia rolls her eyes at me.

ME: Babe, you live in a cramped three bedroom house in Santa Monica, yet you spend millions of dollars on these horses…

OLIVIA: Babe. My horses literally cum diamonds and Ferrari's.
(She points) See that horse? His nickname is "Cazzo d'Oro" (Italian for "The Golden Cock").

Cut to a few weeks later. I'm in Las Vegas on a shoot with a group of pro athletes. After wrap I get a call from a friend of mine.

ENZO: Hey, I saw on Facebook that you're in Vegas. The AVN Awards are going on at the Hard Rock. Swing by. I have a badge for you.

The AVN's are, simply put, the Academy Awards of porn.

ME: I'll meet you for a drink. What could possibly go right?

ENZO: Perfetto. See you soon.

We meet at the Circle Bar on the center of the casino floor. Before long, I'm chatting with a gorgeous and hilarious British adult performer. I'm cruising around with her and meeting new people. Before long, we bump into Keiran Lee, a male adult performer who's from the same area in the Midlands as her. Funny enough, he shares the same nickname as the horse.

ME: So, Keiran. They call you "The Golden Cock," huh?

KEIRAN: Yeah, mate.

ME: Why do they call you that?

KEIRAN: Because I'm the only male performer in the business who can consistently work 28 days per month.

ME: Interesting. How much do you make for a scene?

KEIRAN: Fifteen hundred dollars, mate.

ME: Aren't you married?

KEIRAN: Yeah, mate, but she knows the business. We just have a quick dip.

ME: Y'know, my girlfriend has a horse they also call "The Golden Cock," and he gets like tens of thousands of dollars for an ejaculation.

KEIRAN: Show me dis horse, mate.

I show him the horse's website. He asks me to send it to him. Moments later, he tweets.

"The real Golden Cock. Cazzo d'oro."

I sent the tweet to Olivia.

OLIVIA: I'm screaming laughing right now. I've seen porn with that guy!

"

I will go out of my way to entertain you. To charm you with funny and heartfelt stories to distract you… Do NOT let me.

Chapter Fifty-One

Abandonment Issues

1997, Beverly Hills

In yet another vain attempt to fix my broken brain, I decided to start therapy again. The worst part of starting with a new therapist is having to dredge up an entire lifetime of trauma over a five- to six-month period—which, in and of itself, makes your life worse. Despite my many flaws, I am, if nothing else, self-aware.

On the first day, I warned her:

ME: There are a few things you should know about me before we get started. I will go out of my way to entertain you. To charm you with funny and heartfelt stories to distract you and avoid doing work or feeling anything. Do NOT let me. Be tough.

Dr. Susan thanked me for my honesty, said she understood and would be mindful.

Then the process began. Every horrific trauma that ever happened to me that left me feeling like shit every session over months and months, but knew it was part of the process. At least, that's what I told myself.

We were seven months in when I received a call from her:

DR. SUSAN: Hi. It's Susie!

Susie? I usually called her Doctor plus last name. Never even felt comfortable enough to call her Susan.

ME: Uh. Hello.

DR. SUSAN: I have been doing a lot of thinking and I don't think we can work together any longer.

ME: Why?

DR. SUSAN: It's clear we have developed feelings for each other and I don't think it's a good idea to see each other professionally.

ME: No, we have not developed any feelings. I warned you on the first day to keep me in check. That I would try to charm you, but there was no goal. I do it to everyone. Men, women, young and old.

DR. SUSAN: I think we both know that isn't true, Scott.

ME: (Furious) I'm not saying this to embarrass you, but I've never for a moment thought about you in any way other than as a safe, doctor-patient relationship.

DR. SUSAN: I think we both know that isn't true, Scott.

ME: You'll forgive me if I tell you that I think you need therapy more than I do, and I'm a catastrophe.

DR. SUSAN: Scott. It's over. If you like, I can help you find a new therapist.

ME: What I'd like from you is my money back. I've spent five months and thousands of dollars, and you're abandoning me just as I'm getting into my abandonment issues.

DR. SUSAN: Scott.

ME: Stop saying my name like it's going to soothe me. I'm going to get off the phone before I say a lot of things I really, really mean. This is incredibly unprofessional.

I hung up the call and didn't return to therapy for years.

Three years later, I ran into Dr. Susan at Century City Mall. She was pushing a stroller. We made eye contact. I had moved on, so I smiled and waved. She returned a half smile. I walked over.

ME: Hey, Doc. How are you?

DR. SUSAN: I'm fine.

I couldn't have been more effusive. I looked at her beautiful newborn and asked.

ME: What a beauty! Who's this?

DR. SUSAN: (Without eye contact, clearly uncomfortable) She's my baby.

ME: Meh. Take care, Susie.

66

She had a real knack for it.
In her first seven months,
she made just under
$1,800,000 in cash.

Chapter Fifty-Two

Crêpes Suzette

2022

I was hanging out with this adult film star. I don't say "hanging out" to be coy. I say it because I don't have a better way to describe it. Yes, we had sex sometimes therapeutically, but mostly we were friends. I met her when she reached out via Instagram asking if I'd like to do a photo shoot with her sometime.

She had been in the adult business for the better part of a decade, and was a legit star, doing far better than most. Between shooting scenes and OnlyFans, she was earning between 25 and 45 thousand dollars per month. But, she was burning out and had decided she was finally ready to try escorting and make enough money to implement an exit strategy. Buy a house and figure out an investment plan that would earn her enough passive income to retire for good.

She secured an escort booking agent and was beginning to work. A lot. Since I have one of those faces that everyone tells everything to, I did the best I could to advise her and help keep her safe. She had a real knack for it. In her first seven months, she made just under $1,800,000 in cash.

It's a complex set of emotions to balance real friendship, sex, and having daily discussions about sex with sometimes as many as ten other people in a day, while she circumnavigated the globe on tour.

Her tour stops would generally range between three days for secondary markets like Boston, Philly and Chicago to a week or two in major hubs like New York, Los Angeles and London.

One afternoon she FaceTimed me from the Amman Hotel in New York City. The Amman is the most luxurious hotel chain in the world.

KRISTI: Hey!

ME: Hey! How's everything going there?

KRISTI: Ugh. Remember that Russian oligarch we looked up?

ME: Yeah. Did you see him?

KRISTI: Yeah, but I think he ripped me off.

ME: What do you mean he ripped you off? What did I tell you? You always get the money upfront!

KRISTI: Well, he didn't have any money, so he gave me gold.

ME: What do you mean he gave you gold? Gold jewelry? Gold coins? Gold bars? Ingots? Bullion? What did he give you?

KRISTI: I guess they're bars?

ME: What do they say on them?

KRISTI: They say "Crêpes Suzette."

ME: What?

KRISTI: They say "Crêpes Suzette," Scott!

ME: Ugh. Do you mean, "Credit Suisse?"

KRISTI: Oh… Yes. That.

ME: How much do they weigh?

KRISTI: They say, "One Troy Ounce."

ME: How many did he give you and how much time did you spend with him?

KRISTI: He gave me 12 of them, and he stayed a little under three hours.

ME: You did fine.

KRISTI: How fine?

ME: Gold is trading a little under $1,900 per ounce, so you made a little under $24,000, so kiss the ground.

66

No matter who you are, or what you've achieved in your life, there will always be someone to kick you down the stairs.

Chapter Fifty-Three

LA 101

1999, Malibu

If I learned anything quickly about this town it's that, unlike most cultures, not only is age not exalted, but that they will kick you down the stairs face first, no matter *who* you are.

Example one:

I was at my new boss beach house for a BBQ. It was on Broad Beach which sits at the northernmost point of Malibu's 21 (formerly 27) miles of coastline, at the intersection of Trancas Canyon. It's remote, private and luxurious. I was new in town and enjoying wringing some new hands and meeting people.

BOSS: Scott. Walk with me on the beach. If I don't do it while I'm here, I feel I'm not amortizing the obscene amount of money I spent on this place.

I stood.

BOSS: Ask the boys if they want to join.

I walked over to his son and daughter-in-law. Both in their late 30s. Both born, bred and buttered in Bel-Air. Private schools. Funny and smart, but also very spoiled. As we walked through the back yard toward the sand, I saw an old man in a powder blue cardigan wave.

I reflexively waved back and quietly asked:

ME: Is that Frank Sinatra?

THE SON: Yes. Don't talk to him.

ME: I won't. Is he mean or something?

THE SON: No. He's alright. Just old and crazy and he'll bend your ear all day with his dumb stories.

The balls on this kid. I said nothing, but in that moment, I couldn't think of anything I'd rather do than spending an hour listening to Frances riff stories. By the time we got back from the beach walk, he was already back inside the house.

No matter who you are, or what you've achieved in your life, there will always be someone to kick you down the stairs.

"

He reeked of old New England prep school. Andover or Exeter probably. Like Tucker Carlson without the implausible hairline.

Chapter Fifty-Four

Lil Osc

2022

I had met a new lady friend at a group lunch at a friend's house. She makes her living as a producer and director. The first time we hung out solo, she invited me back to see her new house. I really didn't know much about her and specifically make it a point to not Google people unless it's unavoidable. This includes photo shoots. I like to learn about people organically and through conversation.

The house in Hollywood Hills East was architecturally indistinct, but charming. It was yellow and stucco, but with a normal shingled roof and a white picket fence, oak strip floors and three bedrooms.

As I entered the home, the first thing I noticed was an Academy Award. It's one of those things that no matter how many times you see them they're jarring. Arresting. Unlike other kudocast trophies, the Academy Award is different. Since 1929, as of this writing, there have only been 3,140 Oscars awarded. I haven't won a Golden Globe, Grammy, Tony or Emmy (or even a bowling trophy).

I could tell she was used to this, and handled it in a funny, self-deprecating way:

ALICE: Yes, that *is* an Oscar on an IKEA table. And yes, I'm for certain the poorest Oscar winner of all time.

Solid, self-effacing response.

We became fast friends. Nothing more. She invited me to be her plus-one to the Emmy Awards, which she also won. The Emmy, further to my point above, was a News and Documentary Emmy or, as she called it, a "Nerd Emmy."

We had just returned from the News and Documentary Emmys, AKA Nerd Emmys, at Lincoln Center in New York, and were enjoying Sunday brunch at Soho House West Hollywood, when a guy in his late 20s wearing a suit came over to the table.. Suits aren't really allowed at Soho House, as it's meant to be a community for creatives, not business people.

JUNIOR AGENT: Hey! I'm Trent. I work with your agent, Jim.

We both say a polite hello to the hair gelled, spray tanned, pointy faced weasel. He reeked of old New England prep school. Andover or Exeter probably. Like Tucker Carlson without the implausible hairline.

JUNIOR AGENT: (smirking) Hey, uh I hear you won a little Oscar…

I wanted to rip this kids nuts off. She handled it better.

ALICE: Nooo. It's full sized. What have YOU ever won?

Well played. We gave him one word responses until he skulked away.

To this day, we refer to the golden statue as "Lil Osc."

"

Holly is a woman I briefly dated four years earlier. It didn't work out, and you're about to find out why.

Chapter Fifty-Five

The NuvaRing Incident

2020, Aspen, Colorado

I was on a grouse hunting trip in the mountains with the guys. We found not a single bird, but at least we got to Hemingway cosplay in tweeds and blaze orange hats. We decided to drive into Aspen and meet up for lunch with some old friends of mine.

We were standing outside the crêperie on Hopkins Avenue waiting on our table; when a fit, attractive woman in her late 60s approached in jeans, boots and a white puffer vest over a forest green cashmere turtleneck.

MOM: Excuse me. Are you Scott Nathan?

ME: I am.

MOM: I'm Holly's mother.

Holly is a woman I briefly dated four years earlier. It didn't work out, and you're about to find out why.

ME: Oh, I love Holly! How is she?

MOM: She's doing really well! Whatever happened with you two? You seemed like such a good fit.

I could tell she had a sense of humor and was young at heart. I decided to let it rip.

ME: Well, it was the NuvaRing incident.

One of my guy friends shot me a look.

For those who don't know, the NuvaRing is a vaginally inserted contraceptive device.

MOM: (Cracking up) *What* NuvaRing incident?

ME: One morning, we woke up and I heard this gross noise coming from the floor. When I went to look for it, I noticed my cat Miles had half eaten her NuvaRing. Holly flipped out. She started screaming.

ME: I'll fix it. I promise. I'll pay for a new one.

HOLLY: It's prescription! You can't just *buy* a new one, you stupid motherfucker!

Mom thought the story was hilarious. Three days later, Holly not so much.

"

*I tell the lady I'm apprehensive.
She assures me that once I get
through the first 30 seconds,
it gets easier. It didn't.*

Chapter Fifty-Six

Russell Simmons Froze My Balls

Summer, 2016

M ake me understand this trend of paying a fortune for self-torture like hot yoga, ice baths, cryotherapy, micro needling, microblading, fillers, Botox and dermabrasion?

I'm a sensualist. I loathe discomfort. I'm the guy who changes into pajamas for long-haul flights. I'll do almost anything to be five percent more comfortable. I hate heat and cold. I grew up in Chicago and went to college in Boulder. I'm done with the tundra.

I read an article about a Fortune 100 CEO that kept her own bedding at a dozen of her favorite hotels around the world. The article called her spoiled. To me, it was genius. I don't require luxury, but I think I appreciate it more than most.

I'm spending the afternoon writing at Soho House West Hollywood. Without my distance glasses on, I see, approaching from the distance, a black guy wearing a Yankees cap, flannel shirt and a string of wooden love beads coming into focus from the periphery. That combo could mean only one person.

RUSSELL SIMMONS: Hey, Scott!

Now, I don't know this guy well at all, but he's a dear friend of one of my best friends and we sat across from each other at her birthday dinner years earlier. Enough to say hello when we see each other.

ME: Hey, man! Good to see you. How's everything?

RUSSELL: Great! Don't know if you heard, but I opened a Yoga studio downstairs.

ME: Oh, yeah. I saw an article about it, but didn't realize it was here. It's exciting. Congratulations.

RUSSELL: I'm co-teaching a class in 30 minutes. Come. It's on me.

ME: I'd love to, but I don't have any workout clothes with me.

RUSSELL: We have a shop. Buy a pair of shorts.

ME: OK…

I go downstairs, rifle through my car and find an old pair of board shorts in the trunk. I opt for the Taylor Hawkins/Jeff Spicoli look rather than buying a three-figure pair of yoga shorts.

I enter into the studio and it's Dante's inferno. We gingers don't do well in heat. I exit, purchase two bottles of water, and return. I'm in perpetual back and hip pain with a few herniated discs. I struggle through the class. If I didn't kind of, sort of know the guy, I would've left after 20 minutes. The class ends.

RUSSELL: Scott. Your back is fucked UP.

ME: Russell. Yeah.

RUSSELL: Have you tried cryotherapy?

ME: I've seen the girls do it on Instagram. It looks miserable.

RUSSELL: I've got a place down on La Cienega. It'll help you with your pain and inflammation. Use my name. They wont charge you.

ME: Oh, man. I'll feel like *such* a tool dropping your name.

RUSSELL: Then pay.

I drive there, walk in, and:

ME: Hey, I'm a friend of Russell Simmons…

I put on the strange cryo uniform. Long tube socks to keep the lower legs from frostbite. A surgical mask, gloves, underwear, earmuffs and crocs. They recommend a two-minute session at -240F. All right. Let's just get through this. I tell the lady I'm apprehensive. She assures me that once I get through the first 30 seconds, it gets easier. It didn't.

I exit the freezer place, happy for an 85° degree day. Shivering, I get into my black SUV with tinted windows and turn the seat heaters on ten. It's not helping at all.

I arrive home and draw a hot bath. I spend an hour the tub. I'm warm except for my balls. They feel not only freezing cold, but actually cold to the touch. I took two more baths that night, and two the following day. I'm terrified. The next day, and the day after that, my balls still feel cold. I'm sure I've permanently damaged them with this dumb thing.

Three days later, things were finally back to normal. That evening, I went back to Soho House for a dinner. I entered the sitting room by the fireplace to wait for my guests. I see Russell on the sofa with a group of guys.

ME: Hey, man. Thanks again for yoga the other day. Beautiful spot.

RUSSELL: Glad you liked it. Did you go to Cryo?

ME: I did and wanted to talk to you about that. You froze my balls, Russell!

Russell and his friends look confused and look at me like I'm a crazy person (which I am).

RUSSELL: (Confused, irritated) Scott, what are you talking about?

ME: I'm serious. I think I got frostbite. You need like fleece or cashmere or heated underwear at that place. This shit is dangerous.

He stares blankly at me.

ME: Anyway, good to see you.

ACKNOWLEDGEMENTS

Special Thanks

Parker Bennett *(branding, book, and website design, www.alignedonline.com)*

Madeline Fuhrman at Perfect Ten Media Group
(Kickstarter consultation and merchandise design, www.perfecttenmediagroup.com)

Mosaic Audio

Amy Stoddard
Jim G
Amanda Jane Micallef
Courtney Brooke Wagner
Sarah Dandashy
Summerly & Dan Schulman
Jeff Mincheff
Jeff Levine
L.V.A.
Michael Blatter
Justin Moore
Zooey Deschanel
Jack Osbourne
Dr. Drew Pinsky
Dita Von Teese
Charlotte Sartre
David Kornblum
Alli Cripe at Alli PR
Kirilly Mallard, Australia PR
Heather McDonald & The Juicy Scoopers worldwide

The benevolent ghosts of dead artists at Chateau Marmont
for always helping me push forward

My surrogate families who looked out for me when I needed them,
The Freemans, The Clamans, and The Sheinbergs

Thank You

Jonny Goldstein, Elena Koshka, Anya, Sammy, Dana Harris

PATRONS

"Malibu" Patrons

Summerly and Dan Schulman

"Brentwood" Patrons

Cynthia Fleming

Howard Granat

Michael Lawless

John Supera

"Bel-Air" Patrons

Jon Goldstein

Karen Ross

Courtney Wagner

"Beverly Hills" Patrons

Robert Allen

John Howard

Savannah Ferguson

Justine Freeman

Kelly Redcay

PATRONS

"Hollywood" Patrons

Navah Paskowitz Asner

Adam Bender

Jay Bergman

Lance Bergman

Mario Blenda

Becki Brownell

Angela Bruyere

Leslie Carr

Rebecca Chapman

Rory Collins

Alexander Covarrubias

Kim Dues

Kelly Farmer

Tim Flakoll

Neal Flesner

Bill Foster

Fanny Freeman

Renee Frigo

Joel Garber

Heather Green

Brandon Ray Henderson

Tish Hicks

Theresa Hryckvich

Steve Javors

James Johnson

Erik Lammerding

Luz

Betsy Matz

Melvin Nash

Gary Nugent

Jessica Pelatt

Elizabeth Pigg

Michelle Quisenberry

Karla Ravandi

Layla Revis

Kim Saliba

Wes Siler

Jeff Silvers

Tim & Erin Skold

Jennifer Stevens

Cindy E. Syes

Zita Vass

Jon Vein

Brian Weiss

Joliange Wright

Melissa Wysocki

"LA. It's what's outside that counts."

baddecisionsbook.com/store

ABOUT THE AUTHOR

Scott Michael Nathan is a writer and raconteur living in Los Angeles. He's a top-10 podcast regular and favorite on social media.

Scott is also an award-winning photographer, director, and video artist. His groundbreaking "Confessional" series opened to sellout crowds and critical acclaim at the prestigious Frieze Art Fair in LA in 2019.

baddecisionsbook.com

TikTok @scottnathanphoto
Instagram @scottnathanphoto
Facebook @scottnathanphoto
Twitter @scottnathan